How to select
and use consultants

A client's guide

Management Development Series No. 31

How to select and use consultants

A client's guide

Milan Kubr

International Labour Office   Geneva

Kubr, M.
How to select and use consultants: A client's guide
Geneva, International Labour Office, 1993 (Management Development Series, No. 31)

/Management development/, /Guide/, /Management consultancy/, /Management consultant/, /Selection/. 12.04.1
ISBN 92-2-108517-1
ISSN 0074-6703

ILO Cataloguing in Publication Data

CONTENTS

Figures

Tables

INTRODUCTION

This book has been written for managers and entrepreneurs who are keen to use consultants to improve their management and business performance, but want to know more about effective ways of choosing consultants and working with them.

In the last 20 years, the growth of the consulting industry has been impressive and the range of services that are available from consultants has widened quite considerably. In western Europe and North America the consulting market has turned into a buyers' market: offer exceeds demand and clients can be selective, making sure that they turn to the best expert and get maximum value for their money. Some clients have become real experts in selecting consultants and working with them. However, the know-how involved in choosing and using consultants has not become sufficiently widespread and there are still clients, or potential clients, to whom consulting is a mystery and consultants are suspicious elements. These are the people who view the consultant as someone who borrows your watch to tell you the right time... and then runs away with it.

The developing world has learned about consulting through technical assistance, which has been the principal source of funding of assignments undertaken by the foreign or the emerging local consulting profession. In these countries consulting has been making slow progress, with the exception of a few nations that have managed to industrialize and achieve more rapid economic growth than other countries.

The newest consulting market and the consultants' new frontier is central and eastern Europe. Tremendous demand for consulting services has been created by massive privatization and economic restructuring, and by the strong desire to catch up with western business as quickly as possible. Hundreds of western consulting firms have decided, or are about to decide, that such an opportunity must not be missed. After decades of command economy that stifled individual initiative and suppressed independent and objective professional advice, a local consulting profession started emerging. Its future is very promising. However, the growth and professionalization of consulting in central and eastern Europe are hampered by most clients' lack of experience with consultants. Furthermore, the real professionals have to compete not only among themselves but also with imposters who pretend to be competent consultants although they have hardly anything to offer.

Thus, although the historical settings and the problems faced by the decision-makers are different, in all parts of the world there are businesses and managers who could well make better use of consultants if they knew more about consultant selection and the ways in which consultants can be used.

It would of course be foolish to propose universal rules and standard procedures likely to guarantee success in every single case. Every consulting assignment is unique, and its success depends on many variables that may not exist in other assignments. The chemistry of each consultant-client relationship is extremely complex. However, there are lessons from experience, and sound consulting practices that tend to be followed both by consultants and by experienced users of their services. It should be stressed that, as regards consultants, the real professionals are not interested in collecting large fees for poor service. On the contrary, they enjoy working with well-informed and highly demanding clients, who know what consulting is about, understand the consultant's approach and know how they must collaborate with the consultant. They realize that consulting produces good results if consultants are competent in serving clients and clients in using consultants.

This book is about sound practices of selecting consultants and working with them. Its perspective is international because consulting across national boundaries has become common practice. It deals with consulting to management; therefore the main focus is on those professional services which are known by the terms "management or business consulting". However, business managers and entrepreneurs also seek professional advice from other sources, such as investment bankers helping to find and mobilize capital or negotiate and implement mergers and acquisitions, or law firms advising on legal aspects of business, and many others. Some information on the use of these further sources of expertise and advice to management is therefore included as well.

The structure of this book follows the logic of consultant selection and use. You may be thinking of recruiting a consultant, but before doing that, you certainly want to be well informed about the consulting profession. You want to know about the services offered by consultants, the firms on the consulting market and competition among them, the intervention methods used by excellent consultants, the organization of the profession, and the ethical and quality standards that you can expect from consultants. Chapter 1 will tell you about this.

A consultancy is never an aim in itself, and you will want to be able to determine whether you need a consultant. In Chapter 2, we shall go through all the steps and considerations that precede your decision to recruit one – from problem identification to terms of reference in which you define your needs and describe the task that you intend to entrust to your consultant.

Consultant selection proper is then discussed in two chapters. Chapter 3 will tell you about various criteria that are normally used to find out which consultant will suit you best, and about ways of obtaining and checking information on your candidates. Chapter 4 provides a fairly detailed description of procedures used in selecting consultants.

Costs and fees are an important element in professional services. Since various fee formulas used in consulting are not sufficiently known in client circles, Chapter 5 explains the rationale behind consulting fees and describes principal fee-setting techniques and practices.

Chapter 6 is devoted to consulting contracts. The most common contracting practices are described and some guidance is provided on how to draft a good contract.

We then turn to the use of consultants and to client-consultant interaction and collaboration during assignments. Chapter 7 deals with a number of organizational and procedural issues, such as consultant briefing, work scheduling, progress monitoring and reporting, and interpersonal and behavioural issues, such as the consultant's roles in the change process, and approaches likely to avoid and resolve conflicts and facilitate the transfer of know-how. Chapter 8 looks into various questions that have to be given consideration in winding up a consulting assignment.

Finally, we have found it useful to provide, in Chapter 9, a summary review of the main points made in the book. The purpose of this chapter is to stress those practices thanks to which many clients have become competent users of consulting services. This, after all, is the main purpose of our publication. Therefore the chapter is action oriented and tries to make a few useful suggestions on how to improve the use of consultants.

We assume that some readers will find our book too concise and will start looking for more detailed and specific information on various aspects of consulting. They may wish to turn to *Management consulting: A guide to the profession*,[1] also available from the ILO. The two publications have been conceived as complementary texts: one for those working as consultants and the other one for users of consulting services. After all, looking at consulting and the relationships involved from the other party's perspective can be revealing and stimulating.

The terms "client" and "consultant" are used in this publication as generic terms and relate to clients and consultants in general, regardless of their gender, sector, country and other characteristics. Both terms are used in the masculine gender for the sake of style, although in practice there tend to be more and more women among business people, managers and consultants.

Before turning to the first chapter, the reader may want to have some idea of what a specific consulting assignment looks like. The Biokosma case history should provide such a picture.

---

[1] Edited by Milan Kubr, 2nd (revised) edition, 1986.

Consulting in business strategy at Biokosma

This case history describes a management consulting assignment from a client's perspective. It is based on information provided by Biokosma's managing director Mr. Klaus Erny and the consultant Dr. Peter Beriger. Some of this information was previously published by the Swiss management journal *Der Organisator* (August 1990).

The client organization

Biokosma is a small to medium-sized Swiss company active in health food distribution and biocosmetics. Since its establishment in 1935 the company has been family owned and its founder is still an honorary member of the Board. The Chairman of the Board and the managing director are not members of the family. Legally the enterprise is established as a holding which controls companies in Switzerland and foreign subsidiaries in France and Germany. One company in the holding, Reformhaus Mueller, distributes traditional health foods and operates 22 retail shops, all members of the Swiss health-food distributors' association Biona. This is the field in which Biokosma started its business in the 1930s. One company of the group, Biokosma AG, manufactures and distributes a fairly wide range of biocosmetics, including products for skin, foot and hand care, therapeutical bath products, special soaps and the DUL-X line of sport and health-massage products. Another company, Biorex AG, is an importer and distributor of health foods. The foreign subsidiaries deal with distribution and promotion of Biokosma's products.

The Biokosma Holding AG is registered in Zug. However, the group's principal base is Ebnat-Kappel, a small town in the Toggenburg valley south of St. Gallen. In Ebnat-Kappel the group has its headquarters and Biokosma AG its laboratories, stores, filling and packaging facilities. In 1991, the turnover of the group was 45 million Swiss francs with 210 employees. The manufacturing company Biokosma AG had a turnover of 12 million Swiss francs and employed 50 people.

Since its modest beginnings in 1935, the company's founder and management have viewed service to people's health as Biokosma's principal mission. In the cosmetics business, a deliberate choice has been made to manufacture and sell products based on natural oils and essences. Mineral oils and ingredients have not been used as a matter of technological and product policy. Biokosma is proud of its traditional sensitivity to environmental issues and of its contribution to the protection of the natural environment.

Need for a consultancy

The need to turn to management consultants for help in strategic analysis and new strategy formulation was the result of a number of discussions between the group Chairman (in 1988 new in his position) and the managing director. When the idea was mentioned to him, the company's founder was immediately interested and gave his full support. They all agreed that, in the 1990s, smaller companies in the health products business might have a difficult time in competing with the sector's giants.

Although Biokosma had a business strategy, it was by no means certain that this strategy would pass the test of the difficult business environment of the next decade. In summary, the decision to turn to consultants was motivated by two main reasons: (1) Strategy is about the firm's future. It was therefore worth tapping the best possible expertise that the firm could find and afford, to ensure that the approach taken was the right one and that nothing important had been omitted. (2) In a smaller company, as indeed in many larger businesses, no one in management has special responsibility for, or enough time to think about, future strategy. Everyone is fully occupied running current operations and satisfying customers. Without special efforts and arrangements, the company might never find and allocate enough time to deal with strategic issues seriously.

Consultant selection

Biokosma's Chairman, a retired Swiss businessman, was familiar with the strategy consulting work of a Swiss accounting/consulting firm, ATAG, which belonged to the Ernst and Young international group. ATAG Ernst and Young consultants used a strategy analysis and planning methodology described in an information paper published by the Swiss Volksbank in 1981, and other publications. Both the Chairman and the Managing Director knew about the methodology and found it interesting. Therefore the Chairman contacted ATAG with a request to propose experienced consultants and a suitable approach for the job. After a meeting with management, the consultants came up with an approach, according to which ATAG would provide a methodology and help to apply it in Biokosma, but most of the work would be done by the company itself. Biokosma's management found the approach compatible with its own thinking and agreed to the project. The consultant's proposal was submitted in writing and Biokosma's management gave its agreement verbally.

The approach

The work was to be organized in three phases: diagnosis, strategy formulation and implementation. The bulk of the work, including both legwork and conceptual strategic thinking, would be done by the client's management and staff. For this purpose the client would designate a special project team headed by the managing director. At the beginning and at other critical points in the exercise, the consultants would hold workshop meetings with the project team. These workshops would be used for initial problem review and briefing on the methodology, presenting and reviewing the findings at the end of the diagnostic phase, and examining the proposals for specific strategies developed during the strategy formulation phase. The main presentations at the workshops would be made by the project team, not the consultants. The consultants would ask questions, record new ideas and problems identified, make sure that nothing was overlooked, focus the discussion on key issues and, if appropriate, challenge the conclusions and proposals presented by the project team.

The Biokosma assignment started in 1989 with a strategic workshop meeting involving the project teams of all the Swiss companies of the group. Following this initial meeting, the company project teams started working on strategic analysis. The work concerned both the company (its market position, strengths, weaknesses, future development potential) and the national and international business environment, with special regard to trends, opportunities and competitors in the sectors of health products and cosmetics. This work was completed in eight months. At the end of the diagnostic phase, another series of workshop meetings was held (separately with each company), at which the project teams and the consultants reviewed the results of the diagnosis. The next phase, strategy formulation, took three months. In April 1990, Biokosma was ready to launch the implementation phase.

Start of implementation

The conclusions of the strategy formulation phase were structured as a set of strategic projects. When a particular strategic project was regarded as ready for implementation, management gave the authorization. Thus, implementing strategy was a gradual process. Between 1989 and 1992, several projects were identified, evaluated, approved by management and started. Two of the principal projects concerned the basic strategic position of Biokosma: one aimed at strengthening the firm's leading position in the Swiss market for biocosmetics, while the other focused on building up the international market position of the DUL-X massage products, the firm's leading product line which had the best prospects. Several special projects were approved and launched, such as new market research in two to four countries, a special promotion campaign for the DUL-X massage products through training courses at Swiss sports clubs, the design of a new export concept for DUL-X and further strengthening of the firm's traditionally strong position on environmental protection.

Consultant-client interaction

Biokosma's management regards strategy as the key to the firm's future. If management consultants are called in to help with strategic analysis and planning, this does not imply that the task would be delegated to them. Firstly, consultants cannot possess the knowledge and know-how that are acquired by years of experience in the sector. Secondly, even if they had such experience and were able to produce the best strategic ideas and plans, these might be ignored and even sabotaged by management and staff members who have not been involved in the exercise. Motivation for implementing strategy develops in the course of strategy formulation.

Biokosma has no detailed records of the time spent by its management and staff on the consulting project. According to rough estimates, management spent ten times longer than the consultants on strategy analysis and planning, not including time taken for strategy implementation.

Direct interaction between management and the consultants took place mainly at the project team level, during workshop meetings and additional individual contacts. Other employees were involved case by case, e.g. by collecting and analysing data on products, costs, customers or competitors. Information on the project and the progress made was widely disseminated throughout the company.

It became quickly evident in the course of the exercise how important it was for the person at the top to have the right attitude. The project enjoyed the enthusiastic support of the group's and Biokosma's management. In the health-food distribution sector, the manager in charge of Biorex at that time did not believe in the necessity of the exercise and was not prepared to work at making it a success. Therefore the results in this sector were less satisfactory and some strategic projects were not implemented. The manager had to be replaced and a new manager was recruited with the help of ATAG's executive search division. In Reformhaus Mueller, the management team had to be strengthened in the area of marketing and sales.

Follow-up

The assignment carried out under the first agreement with ATAG was limited to 12 days of consultancy by a team of two experts in corporate strategy (24 days, later extended to 30 days in total). It was completed in 1990. Since then, the consultants have returned to Biokosma for several short meetings to review progress and outstanding problems. In addition, the leading ATAG consultant who in 1989 started the work with Biokosma was invited to become a member of the group's Board of Directors (a practice that is not uncommon in Switzerland). This is a retainer arrangement for eight days per year, for which ATAG receives a fee.

Owing to recent changes in both the business environment and within Biokosma, the firm's management is considering repeating a series of strategic review meetings in 1992-93. The rationale behind this is the feeling that strategy should be reviewed from time to time and brought up to date. It is true that this cannot be done every month, but it should be done frequently enough to make sure that the strategy chosen is still valid and does not become outdated. Consultants might be brought in again, probably for shorter interventions. They may come with new ideas and suggest improved methodologies for diagnosis and other tasks. In addition, the consultants' presence may once again give Bioskosma the impetus to give strategic issues the attention they deserve.

Conclusion

The Biokosma case is neither special, nor spectacular. It shows (a) that a relatively small assignment in terms of consultant work-days can be of help in dealing with critical management issues, (b) that management's involvement, motivation and leadership are essential, and (c) that a small or medium-sized company can also afford to use external consultants if the assignment is well designed and managed.

ON CONSULTING AND CONSULTANTS

1

This opening chapter provides an overview of the consulting profession and the market for consulting services. To a new user of consulting services, it will give basic information on what consulting is about, how consultants operate, how the consulting market functions and what professional standards are regarded as normal practice in consulting. A reader who is more experienced in using consultants may be familiar with the basics given in the first part of the chapter (sections 1.1 and 1.2). However, even an experienced client may find useful information in sections 1.3 to 1.5, which will update his knowledge of trends in the consulting market, relations between consultants and various other suppliers of consulting and similar services, and problems faced in applying professional standards.

1.1. What can management consultants do for you?

Who is a consultant?

Let us start by looking at some general characteristics of consultants. The term "consultant" is generic and can be applied to any person or organization that provides advice to decision-makers. This advice can take many different forms and concern any area of human activity and interests: there are consultants on pension plans, garden layout, buying antiques and raising funds for social organizations. Anyone who feels like it can call himself a consultant – if he finds people willing to listen to him.

The terms "management consultant" or "business consultant" point to the area of the consultant's intervention, which is assistance to entrepreneurs, managers and other decision-makers in business and management, in both the private and public sectors. In most countries it is not an officially defined and protected title. Anyone who believes that he has something to offer to managers can position himself as a management consultant. Clients looking for management advice can choose from a wide range of service offerings by consultants who exhibit tremendous differences in background, experience, competence, work styles, conditions of intervention, quality of service and professional standards. Therefore no client can escape from the time-consuming, risky and sometimes painful task of selecting the right consultant. The consultant's profile must be matched to the nature of the problem at hand and the client's specific requirements. In addition, the wheat has to be separated from the chaff.

In our conception (which will be used consistently in this publication) the consultant is a person or organization that meets the following four criteria.

1. The consultant offers and provides something that the client is lacking, but wishes to acquire in various areas of business and management knowledge, expertise, experience or know-how. It can be a special and narrow subject, such as job evaluation for clerical occupations, or a broad and multidisciplinary topic, such as diagnosing companies in difficulties. It can be state-of-the-art expertise in information technology applications or international financial markets, or conventional down-to-earth know-how on improving the organization of small maintenance shops. When working for a client, the consultant will give undivided, 100 per cent attention to the problem at hand – something that a busy manager or administrator can seldom afford.

2. The consultant is someone who knows how to work with clients in helping to identify and solve their problems. He realizes that clients have varying needs and personalities, and are more or less experienced in using consultants. Therefore the consultant uses various methodological tools for helping the client to define problems and analyse their causes, recognize the need for change, choose among alternatives, overcome psychological and other barriers to change, and implement the right decisions. To a certain extent, every consultant must have psycho-sociological and communication skills in addition to being an expert in production control, employee compensation or any other special area of management.

3. The consultant is an independent and objective adviser. He must be able and willing to tell his client the truth and give a totally independent and unbiased opinion without having to worry about any possible consequences to the consultant as a person and the consulting firm that employs him. He should be independent of the client himself, any supervising authority, organizations and people who have or would like to have a business stake in the client organization, centres of political power in the community and so on. Most consulting firms are owned by the consultants themselves and are fully independent. Some firms are owned by banks, governments, or other professional or business firms and agencies. In these cases it is necessary to make sure that the firm's ownership pattern does not constrain independence and objectivity in any way.

4. The consultant is someone who has chosen to abide by a professional code of ethics and conduct. We shall see that it may be an official code of a

consulting association where the consultant is a member, or a personal code defined by the consultant himself. It is important that there is no misunderstanding between the consultant and the client about the interpretation of this code and the consultant's behaviour. The client-consultant relationship is based on trust above all. In particular, the client must feel sure that the consultant is absolutely honest with him and that serving the client's interest is the guiding principle of the consultant's behaviour.

Management and business consultants exhibit many other characteristics. However, the four above-mentioned characteristics – technical competence, consulting know-how, independence and professional integrity – are the core characteristics of professional consultants.

Conversely, there are characteristics about which a lot has been written, although they are less important. Some observers of consulting recognize only those professionals as real consultants who do consulting for a living or devote to it at least 50-60 per cent of their time. In certain contexts these criteria are meaningful. However, if you are a client looking for the best possible advice, do you really care whether the expert of your choice does consulting full or part time?

The professional and the commercial side of consulting

A small amount of consulting may be available free or at subsidized prices. For example, some small business advisory services provide the first consultation (say, half a day) free to a new client, or some governments (e.g. Germany, Singapore, United Kingdom) have introduced schemes through which they subsidize and encourage the use of consultants by small firms. However, in most cases a client who wants to use the consultant must purchase his service and pay a market price for it. Consulting firms are sellers of professional services and clients are buyers. This creates a double relationship between the client and the consultant – professional and commercial. Throughout this book, we shall pay considerable attention to this double relationship. Our purpose will be to show how to balance the professional and the commercial side in choosing consultants, defining and respecting mutual commitments, signing consulting contracts and working with consultants during assignments.

Turning to the consultant, he has to balance the professional and the commercial sides in running the consulting firm. He has to pursue both professional and commercial objectives. Clients need to obtain a professional service of high technical quality and must be able to trust the consultant's integrity. At the same time, the consultant runs a commercial operation and has to worry about issues such as costs and prices, liquidity, interest rates, profit margins, remuneration levels able to attract and retain talented professionals, and so on.

Being an informed client also implies some insight into this "chemistry" of a professional firm. For example, excessive price-cutting in order to win new clients can land the consultant into serious financial difficulties and almost certainly will prevent him from investing in expanding the firm's knowledge base. Conversely, overcharging and taking advantage of the clients' limited knowledge of consulting practices is unprofessional and cannot be excused by any arguments.

Areas of management consulting services

Management consultants provide a wide range of services on virtually all aspects of managing and running businesses of any size and complexity, and on management and administration in governmental and not-for-profit organizations. They aim to be at the forefront of the state of the art of management and to be versed in those issues with which management is struggling, and is likely to be struggling in the next months and years.

Take the current dramatic changes in central and eastern European economies. Thousands of enterprises are preparing and implementing privatization programmes, restructuring their total business and looking for new strategies, in many cases involving mergers, acquisitions or alliances with foreign business partners. The management consulting profession has perceived these changes as a challenge and an unprecedented opportunity to offer services in areas that are new to most managers; hence the important role played by consultants in privatization and restructuring, including issues such as company valuation, search for new partners, redesign of accounting and control systems, application of information technology, staff retraining and so on. These are priority issues not only in central and eastern Europe, but in many other countries aiming to restore and strengthen market economies.

Other examples could be given. All over the world managers face challenges such as improving environmental protection, keeping pace with progress in information technology, taking advantage of developments in telecommunications and understanding what global competition and internationalization of business mean to their firm. The changes in the business and management environment stimulate developments in managerial concepts, techniques and practices, leading to the development of concepts and techniques as different as risk management, local area networks, electronic mail, action learning, management buy-outs or total quality management. Consultants aim to keep abreast of these developments (some of which even have their origin in the work of leading consulting firms), helping clients to find new responses to the challenges of a business environment where continuous change is the only constant.

Table 1.1 gives a listing of activity areas of management consultants used by the European Federation of Management Consulting Associations (FEACO). It also shows areas where most of the work was performed in 1992 in Europe. Data from the United States point to an even larger share of consulting in information technology (over 35 per cent) and in human resource management, including employee benefits and compensation (about 30 per cent).

Table 1.1. Areas of management consulting activity (% in 1992)

Technical area	Europe
Corporate strategy and organization development	23.6
Financial and administrative systems	9.6
Human resources	8.7
Production and services management (incl. technology, logistics, R & D, and quality control)	24.4
Marketing and corporate communication	7.1
Information technology and systems	17.2
Project management	7.0
Economic and environmental studies	2.4

Source: *1993 FEACO Survey* (unpublished material).

How clients use consultants

Clients use their consultants in various ways depending on the situational context. We have found it useful to group these ways under eight headings as shown in table 1.2 and discussed below.

Extending staff

A consultant can be used to supplement the organization's staff. Long-term recruitment can thus be avoided since the consultant will leave the organization when the job has been completed. Usually these consultants will be specialists in areas such as information technology, job evaluation, office administration, and so on. At times consultants are recruited to occupy a vacant position in the management hierarchy on a temporary basis. Although this is not the most typical way of using a consultant, it has been found useful by companies seeking an executive or looking for an interim staffing arrangement.

Table 1.2. How clients use consultants – Checklist

(1) **Extending staff**
If you lack time and sufficient staff to tackle a problem.

(2) **Acquiring information**
If you lack information on environment, competition, business and technology trends or other matters needed to make correct plans and decisions.

(3) **Establishing new business contacts and linkages**
If you need help in finding suitable business contacts and negotiating deals with them.

(4) **Obtaining an impartial expert opinion**
If you need an opinion independent of your own, formally or informally.

(5) **Identifying, diagnosing and solving problems**
If you need help with any aspect and at any stage of problem diagnosis and solving, including overall diagnosis of your business.

(6) **Developing and implementing new methods and systems**
If you want to modernize your planning, scheduling, control, management information and other systems.

(7) **Planning and implementing organizational change**
If you need a professional change agent to help design and implement an effective change strategy and overcome barriers to change.

(8) **Training and developing management and staff**
If you want to apply experience and know-how that is best acquired through training.

(9) **Any combination of (1) to (8)**
If you want to enhance impact by combining two or more items described above.

Acquiring information

In many situations, better, more complete and reliable information is all that is wanted from a consultant. It can be information needed to assess a potential new market, or to compare the performance of your organization with that of a similar organization in another country. If you obtain such information, you may be able to draw your own conclusions. The assumption is, of course, that the consulting firm already possesses such information in its data banks and files or can collect it for you using ways and means that you cannot or do not wish to use. For example, a consultant could be recruited to perform a market survey or customer opinion research. He will collect information, evaluate it and present it to the client for consideration. The information function of consultants is important, since many clients, especially the smaller businesses, find it difficult to systematically collect and screen all information that may be important to their business.

Establishing new business
contacts and linkages

Some clients turn to consultants in their search for new business contacts, agents, representatives, suppliers, subcontractors, joint-venture and merger partners, companies for acquisition and so forth. The consultant's tasks may involve identifying one or more suitable persons or organizations, presenting their names to the client, assessing their suitability, recommending a choice, and acting as an intermediary and/or facilitator in preparing and negotiating the deal. Often these contacts would be in other countries than the client's own, and not sufficiently known to the client.

Obtaining an impartial
expert opinion

Thanks to his independence and objectivity, a professional consultant is in a position to give decision-makers an impartial opinion in cases where different choices could be made and management feels that its own position, or the views expressed by experts on the company's staff, cannot be impartial. In other words, the consultant's expertise is being sought in order to confront, assess, evaluate and possibly correct the client's own expertise.

A consultant's impartial opinion can be sought for various reasons: for example, to obtain an expert opinion on the soundness of a major decision faced by management, or as a sounding-board whereby management periodically reviews important issues with a respected consultant before taking a decision. Any consultancy involves an element of the consultant's impartial and unbiased opinion in situations where management decisions risk being affected by a lack of expertise, incomplete information, company myopia or vested interests.

Identifying, diagnosing and
solving problems

Diagnostic skills and instruments are among consultants' principal assets. Clients therefore use consultants for a wide range of diagnostic functions: to diagnose the company and assess its strengths and weaknesses; to analyse industry and market trends, and assess the company's competitive position; and to identify and analyse problems in a specific area of management. Diagnosis can be comprehensive and cover the entire business, or be focused on a narrow problem. It may be the only task for which a consulting contract has been signed. The client will decide what action to take, and either pursue the project without the consultant, or ask the consultant to come up with proposals for appropriate solutions. The consultant will then work on these solutions and propose one or more alternatives.

Developing and implementing
new methods and systems

A wide range of consultant interventions are grouped under this heading. Many clients use consultants to modernize their organizational, recording, planning and control methods and systems, which can be in any area and function of management. The systems can be custom-made (i.e. specially developed for the client) or standard (i.e. delivered and introduced by the consultant with or without adaptation). Increasingly, consultants use proprietary systems, for which the consulting firm holds copyright or is authorized by the holder of copyright to sell the system as part of its services. The degree of the consultant's involvement can vary from case to case. Many organizations prefer to retain the consultant until the system becomes fully operational and achieves the promised parameters.

Planning and implementing
organizational change

A fairly common case is that of a client who may possess the technical and managerial expertise to run the organization, but has difficulties and feels insecure when organizational changes are anticipated and cannot be avoided. Often these changes will put a lot of strain on people, since deep-rooted relationships, work habits and individual or group interests will be affected. In such situations, the expertise sought from a consultant would be in change management – in identifying the need for change, developing a change strategy, choosing and applying the right approaches to encourage change and overcome barriers to change, monitoring the change process, evaluating the progress made and results obtained and adjusting the approach taken by management at all stages of the change cycle. The consultant may provide expertise and advice both on specific methods and techniques that are being changed, and on how to deal with interpersonal relations, conflicts, motivation, team building and other issues in the field of organizational and human behaviour. In Chapter 7, the consultant's functions in supporting change in the client organization will be discussed in more detail. The weight put on behavioural skills will be higher in assignments where resistance to change can be expected and management feels that its own change management skills are inadequate.

Training and developing
management and staff

Training is one of the universal tools for increasing knowledge and skills. In consulting, training is normally provided in conjunction with and in support of other work done by the consultant. The client and his staff are trained in the new methods and techniques introduced by the consultant, so that they become autonomous in using and even improving them. There are many ways in which consulting and training are combined in practice.

Training can also be organized instead of the other interventions and ways of using consultants described above. It may be the client's deliberate choice. Rather than asking a consultant to work on a specific diagnostic, problem-solving or change management assignment, the client may prefer the consultant to prepare and conduct a course or a workshop for managers and/or staff specialists on the subject area where the assignment would have taken place. For example, a set of workshops on productivity improvement is organized instead of requesting the consultant to identify specific productivity improvement measures and present a productivity improvement programme.

Why are consultants used?

Let us now look at the most common reasons, or driving forces, behind these various uses of management consultants.

Curiosity

Whether they admit it or not, some managers do not pursue any clearly defined purpose when inviting a consultant to their organization. They invite him because he is a star or has a reputation of someone who succeeds where everyone has come to grief. So why not try? "Let us see what he can achieve in our difficult setting. Maybe he will tell us something we do not know... After all, even if nothing comes of it, we can afford the luxury of having an outstanding expert with the company for few days!"

Insecurity

Insecurity is a more common reason. A manager may feel insecure because of lack of information, growing criticism and unrest within the company, increasingly aggressive competition, age, fragile personal health or for another reason. Turning to a consultant is then a measure of relief – like hoping that a doctor will tell us that we are not really sick and, if we are, will help us to recover.

To have an alibi

In recruiting a consultant, some managers seek an alibi. They want to be able to refer to an external expert authority in justifying a decision, especially if it will be an unpopular one, likely to generate resistance or criticism; or a manager may want to show that he is aware of the problem and has already looked into it seriously – as witnessed by a consultant's report (as a rule, no action will be taken on such a report).

Improved business results

Fortunately, in the vast majority of cases, the use of consultants is clearly motivated by management's will to improve organizational performance and business results. This is the principal and overriding reason. The manager's immediate objective may be to prevent current performance from slipping, take corrective measures if performance has deteriorated, or use the consultant for future-oriented work such as analysing trends, identifying opportunities and developing medium- and longer-term strategies. The common denominator will be the same – bottom-line results and improved performance.

Learning

In the modern philosophy of consulting, the client's learning is increasingly regarded as a significant reason justifying the use of consultants. Assignments pursue a double purpose: to solve a specific problem by applying the consultant's expertise, and to transfer this expertise to managers and specialists in the client company. Learning may even be the only immediate motive of an assignment if, as mentioned above, the consultant is recruited to run a training course in a client organization and the client decides to take care of other work involved in using the results of that course for making practical improvements. Alternatively, the consultant may be recruited so that the client can observe and learn the consultant's diagnostic and problem-solving methodology at work, compare it with his own and choose which is best. Clients increasingly turn to consultants not to find a solution to one distinct problem, but to acquire the consultant's special technical knowledge and learn the skills used in solving problems and implementing change.

The trend towards participative consulting

Learning from consulting is not automatic. A lot of money has been spent on assignments from which clients have learned very little. If your objective is to use consulting for developing your own and your collaborators' competence, there is only one way in which this can be achieved: through active participation and collaboration in consulting assignments. If you sign a contract and expect the consultant to do the job by himself, without your participation, there will be no learning effect. Furthermore, if the client does not participate, the consultant's task is much more difficult. True enough, the client leaves him in peace and the consultant can proceed with the job without being bothered. No one is breathing down his neck. However, there are more drawbacks than advantages. The consultant gets no feedback, no help, and has to take many decisions on matters concerning the client without being able to check on how the client feels about it. The moment of truth comes at the end, when the project is finished. If the client is not happy, it is too late. The client feels no commitment to the solution proposed by the consultant. It is the consultant's solution and the client does not feel like its "owner". He may explicitly reject the consultant's proposals, or accept them reluctantly only intending to implement them with substantial changes. Clearly, this sounds like an extremely wasteful way of using costly expertise.

In a nutshell, consulting deserves to be called participative if:

o   the assignment is designed jointly by the consultant and the client;

o   the assignment design and plan specify when, in what way and for how long the client's staff will contribute to the task at hand;

o   the consultant is not used for tasks that the client can do, except if this is justified by a shortage of staff time or other well-defined reasons;

o   the progress of the assignment is frequently reviewed, important questions are examined jointly, and the assignment plan and methodology are flexibly adjusted with a view to increasing the client's involvement;

o   specific information, briefing and training sessions are provided to prepare the client for active participation;

o   the consultant encourages and applies a collaborative and participative style of work at all levels of the client organization's structure.

The best test will be your feeling at the end of the assignment. Do you feel that the consultant has delivered a good product, although you are not quite sure if it could be fully applied? Or do you feel that you, with your team and valuable assistance from a consultant, have done exactly what the situation required, and jointly found the best possible solution to your problem?

1.2. What happens during a consulting assignment?

We have seen that management consultants provide a wide range of expertise and do many different things. Therefore generalizing about their modes of operation and giving standard models of their assignments is somewhat risky. Yet it is useful for a client to know what approaches and methods are practised in modern consulting. If your consultant proposes to work in a different way, you may wish to compare the proposed approach with the patterns that prevail in consulting. Maybe your consultant has an innovative approach and his contribution will be particularly valuable. It can also happen that your consultant's proposed approach is inadequate. You will want to find this out before it is too late. This section is limited to a general overview of the consulting process and the consultant's roles. We shall return to these questions many times and in more detail in the following chapters.

Most consulting work in management is done through assignments (also called engagements, cases, client accounts, or projects). An assignment can be simple and small and require only a couple of hours of the consultant's time, or complex, of considerable size, requiring months or even years of work of an important consultant team. In a typical assignment, the consultant agrees with the client to do a particular job over a defined period of time. The client and the consultant reach agreement on an objective to be achieved, the sort of work to be done, the expertise to be provided by the consultant, the client's participation in the assignment, the resources required, the timetable, the price to be paid and various other conditions. This is then summarized and confirmed in a consulting contract.

An alternative to an assignment covering a distinct task and period of time is a retainer. Under a retainer contract, the client books, or purchases in advance, a certain amount of the consultant's working time. The work to be done is defined in general terms only and will be specified at the beginning of each period covered by the contract. For example, the client may use the consultant's services for two days every month during the first week of the month, and review with him the general situation of the business, the problems that have developed during the previous month and the key decisions that will have to be taken.

The consulting process

During a typical assignment, the consultant and the client undertake a set of activities required for planning and implementing the desired changes. These activities are normally known as the consulting process. To describe the consulting process we shall use a simple five-phase model taken from the ILO guide to the management consulting profession.[1] The model, shown in figure 1.1, includes the following phases: entry – diagnosis – action planning – implementation – termination. Other models can be found in the literature, but their difference from our model is semantic (different terms are used) or structural (the process is broken down into a greater number of phases). The basic logic remains the same.

1. Entry

In this phase the consultant starts working with a client. This includes their first contacts, discussions on what the client would like to change in his organization and how the consultant may help, the clarification of their respective roles, the preparation of an assignment plan based on preliminary

---

Figure 1.1. Phases of the consulting process

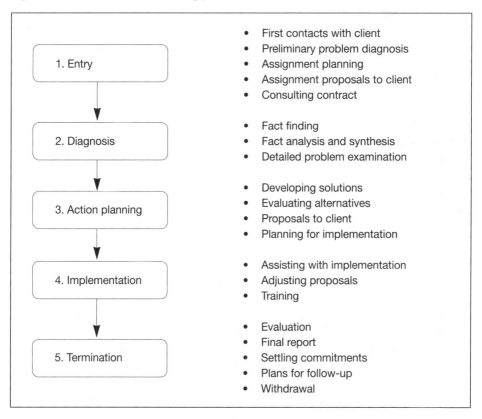

problem analysis, and the negotiation and signing of a consulting contract. It is a preparatory and planning phase. Nevertheless, it lays down the foundations for everything that will follow, since the subsequent phases will be strongly influenced by the quality of the conceptual work done, and by the kind of relationships that the consultant is able to establish with his client at the very beginning.

At this initial phase it can also happen that an assignment proposal is not prepared to the client's satisfaction, or that several consultants are invited to present proposals, but only one of them is selected for the assignment and gets the contract.

2. Diagnosis

The second phase is an in-depth diagnosis of the problem to be solved, based on thorough fact finding and fact analysis. During this phase the consultant and the client cooperate at identifying the sort of change that is required. Is the fundamental change problem technological, organizational, informational, psychological or other? If it has all these dimensions, which is the crucial one? What attitudes to change prevail in the organization: is the need for change appreciated, or will it be necessary to persuade people that they will have to change? The results of the diagnostic phase are summarized and conclusions drawn on how to orient work on action proposals so that the real problem is resolved and the desired benefits obtained. Some possible solutions may start to emerge.

Fact finding and fact diagnosis often receive the least attention. Yet decisions on what data to look for and what data to omit, what aspects of the problem to examine in depth and what aspects to skip, predetermine the relevance and quality of solutions that will be proposed. Also, by collecting data the consultant is already influencing the client organization, and people may start changing as a result of the consultant's presence.

3. Action planning

The third phase aims at finding the solution to the problem. It includes work on alternative solutions, the evaluation of alternatives, the elaboration of a plan for implementing changes and the presentation of proposals to the client for decision. Action planning requires imagination and creativity, as well as a rigorous and systematic approach in identifying and exploring feasible alternatives, eliminating proposals that could lead to trivial and unnecessary changes, and deciding what solution will be adopted. The consultant can choose from a wide range of techniques, in particular if the client's participation in this phase is active. A significant dimension of action planning is developing strategy and tactics for implementing changes, in particular for dealing with those human problems that can be anticipated, and for overcoming resistance to change.

4. Implementation

Implementation, the fourth phase of consulting, provides an acid test of the relevance and feasibility of the proposals developed by the consultant in collaboration with his client. The new system is finalized, developed in detail and put into effect. The changes proposed start to become a reality. Things begin happening, either as planned or differently. Unforeseen new problems and obstacles may arise and false assumptions or planning errors may be uncovered. Resistance to change may be quite different from what was assumed at the diagnostic and the planning stage. The original design and action plan may need to be corrected. As it is not possible to foresee exactly every relationship, event or attitude, and the reality of implementation often differs from the plan, monitoring and managing implementation is very important. This also explains why professional consultants prefer to be associated with the implementation of changes that they have helped to identify and plan.

This is an issue over which there has been much misconception and misunderstanding. Many consulting assignments end when a report with action proposals is transmitted, i.e. before any implementation starts. If the client is fully capable of handling any phase of the change process by himself, and is keen to do it, there is no reason why he should keep a consultant. The consultant may leave as soon as he has completed diagnostic work. Unfortunately, the decision to terminate the assignment before starting implementation often does not reflect the client's assessment of his own capabilities and his determination to implement the proposals without any further help from the consultant. Rather it mirrors a widespread misconception about consulting according to which consultants do not have to achieve more than getting their reports accepted by the clients. Some clients accept this because they have not really understood that even a very solid consulting report cannot guarantee that a new scheme will work and that the promised results will be attained. Other clients (those looking for an alibi) may be happy with this solution because all they really wanted was a report, not a change.

5. Termination

The fifth and final phase in the consulting process includes several activities. The consultant's performance during the assignment, the approach taken, the changes made and the results achieved have to be evaluated by both the client and the consulting organization. Final reports are presented and adopted. Mutual commitments are settled. If there is an interest in pursuing the collaborative relationship, an agreement on follow-up and future contacts may be negotiated. Once these activities are completed, the consultant withdraws from the client organization and the assignment is terminated by mutual agreement.

The consultant's roles in the process

As a general rule, consultants aim never to forget that they are advisers and helpers, not decision-makers. Their purpose is to help the client to make and implement the right decisions, not to take decisions on the client's behalf. The consulting profession has developed various models of consulting for achieving this general purpose. These models involve quite different consultant behaviours in relating to the client and collaboration with him at various stages of the assignment.

Take an example of business strategy, an area where consultants intervene quite frequently. Consultant A will interview the client, collect the data and reports from marketing, planning and accounting departments, gather further

---

information on market trends, export possibilities, competition, technology, raw material prices and so on. Then he will work out a strategy, possibly in several alternatives, which will be presented to the client for review and selection.

Consultant B will tackle the same assignment differently. In his approach to consulting, the best thing is not to deliver a finished product packaged in a nicely presented report, but to stimulate and support the client so that he himself develops the same (and hopefully a better) product. Most of the work will be done by the client. The consultant will limit himself to helping in the diagnosis, giving feedback to the client and making him aware of the processes that are taking place in the organization, the attitudes and the behaviour of the people involved, the influence of organizational traditions and culture on the process of strategic analysis and planning, the mistakes that have been made and their causes, and so on. Furthermore, when necessary, the consultant will provide specific technical inputs whenever the process risks stalling as a result of a lack of technical knowledge, information or know-how. There are several reasons behind this approach, but three of them are particularly important.

The first reason is the client's attitude to the assignment and its outcome: solutions prepared by outsiders, without any client participation, do not get the same support and treatment as solutions that people in the client organization develop, understand, accept and support as their own conception and solution of the problem and the product of their own effort. Expressed in other terms, the client has to "own" the solution of the problem, and to own it in the psychological sense of the term he must develop it himself, not buy it from a consultant as a finished product.

The second reason is learning: if the client receives a final product from the consultant and is told what to do about it, he and his people have been deprived of an excellent opportunity to learn in working with the consultant.

The third reason is pursuit of effectiveness in using company resources: as a rule, clients can and want to do many things involved in a consulting assignment, although the job in its totality may be beyond their competence, at least at the present time. In addition, there is a lot of wisdom and know-how in every organization, which an external consultant can tap not by interviewing but only by enlisting people's active participation in the assignment. In many organizations, the problem is not lack of competence among its staff, but poor communication and collaboration, and insensitive management. Competence is dormant and people do not bother to submit proposals for improvement, being convinced that management is not interested.

Consultant A's behavioural role is described as an expert (resource, content) role (or model) of consulting. The consultant provides the special technical expertise, does the job and suggests to the client the decision to take. The client accepts or rejects this suggestion.

Consultant B's behavioural role is described as a process mode of consulting because it focuses on diagnosing and improving processes whereby the client organization makes and implements decisions. These processes can concern the "hard" side of management (applying the right sequence and combination of techniques in data collection and analysis, needs and opportunities assessment, etc.) or its "soft" side (interpersonal relations, motivation, sharing of information, collaboration and other people-related processes within the organization).[2] The client cannot reject the solutions thus developed because he himself is their principal author, while the consultant was involved as a helper and a catalyst.

It is obvious that the choices concerning the consultant's roles have direct implications for the client's roles. The consultant's and the client's roles are communicating vessels. If the consultant does all the work, he forces the client into the role of a passive observer with all the risks and inefficiencies involved. Conversely, if the consultant expects initiative and specific technical inputs from an unprepared and inexperienced client, the project may halt owing to lack of direction and proper communication. It should be stressed that, in their own interest, the consultant and the client should be able and willing to discuss and vary their roles in the course of an assignment to make the best use of both the consultant's expertise and the client's own potential.

An alternative perspective

David Maister has provided another perspective for explaining the roles played by consultants in serving clients. His allegoric model, reproduced in figure 1.2, includes four prototypes of intervention patterns characteristic of various consulting firms:

○ A consultant practising "surgery", or even "brain surgery", is an outstanding expert and intervenes individually or in a small team of professionals of equally high level. Usually he is faced with very difficult if not critical situations requiring quick, radical and highly competent interventions to restructure or turn around a company, achieve major cost reductions, find a takeover partner, remove incompetent senior management and so on. The client has little choice and trusts the consultant. The client's participation may be limited or nil. Surgery is practised under anaesthetic in most cases and an unconscious patient cannot be expected to participate.

○ A consultant intervening in a "psychotherapy" or a "family doctor" mode is similar to the process consultant (consultant B) as described above. He may face an equally complex and difficult problem as the surgeon, but the approach taken will be different. With patience, methodically and step by step, the consultant will help the client to dissect the

Figure 1.2. A model of professional service firms

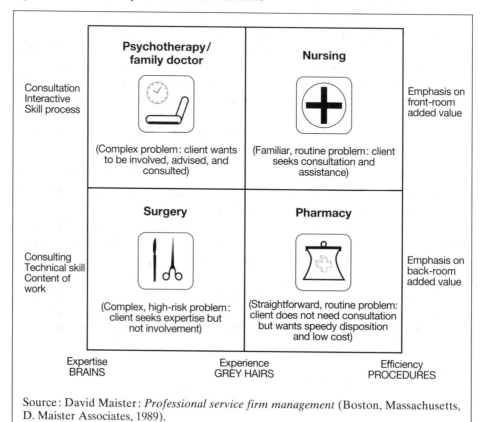

Consultation
Interactive
Skill process

**Psychotherapy/
family doctor**

(Complex problem: client wants
to be involved, advised, and
consulted)

Nursing

(Familiar, routine problem: client
seeks consultation and
assistance)

Emphasis on
front-room
added value

Consulting
Technical skill
Content of
work

Surgery

(Complex, high-risk problem:
client seeks expertise but
not involvement)

Pharmacy

(Straightforward, routine problem:
client does not need consultation
but wants speedy disposition
and low cost)

Emphasis on
back-room
added value

Expertise
BRAINS

Experience
GREY HAIRS

Efficiency
PROCEDURES

Source: David Maister: *Professional service firm management* (Boston, Massachusetts, D. Maister Associates, 1989).

problem, uncover and understand forces hampering change, agree on the best treatment, and provide the patient with advice and help as long as necessary, until he recovers his health and full strength.

o   A consultant who carries out "nursing" will have a client who does not face particularly difficult problems, but is not very sure of himself, needs someone to act as sounding-board, "hold his hand" and increase his self-confidence. From time to time, the consultant may provide missing information and give advice on various matters. He will need to be skilful and tactful to make sure that the client does not become used to always having a consultant behind him. Indeed, the purpose is not to provide nursing on a permanent basis.

o   A consultant who has chosen the "pharmacy" model can provide two sorts of drugs: standard systems and techniques that can be used in a wide range of client firms, and custom-made systems designed for specific clients (or developed by adapting standard systems). Usually this

Table 1.3. Consultant intervention techniques

(1)   **Finding and providing management and business information**
(for the client to use or ignore; the consultant can be responsive and answer questions, or pro-active, selecting and giving information that the client should know)

(2)   **Performing the client's task**
(instead of the client, who may choose to be involved or not; as a rule a consultant would not be used for routine tasks)

(3)   **Delivering systems and methodologies**
(proposing and helping to introduce systems and methodologies developed by the consulting firm or purchased on the market)

(4)   **Demonstrating and teaching how to do a job**
(showing and helping the client to master an improved method)

(5)   **Diagnosing the client's condition**
(helping the client to become aware of strengths, weaknesses, market position and development potential on the basis of hard data)

(6)   **Telling the client what to do**
(so-called advocacy, if the client wants the the consultant to make a choice, or if the client is indecisive at a critical moment)

(7)   **Presenting alternatives with recommendations**
(the consultant recommending the best alternative, leaving the final choice to the client)

(8)   **Presenting alternatives without recommendations**
(same as 7, without recommendations)

(9)   **Asking questions to stimulate thinking and action**
(bluntly or softly drawing the client's attention to existing or missed opportunities, available choices, needed decisions, idle resources, etc.)

(10) **Observing organizational processes and giving feedback**
(making the client aware of strong and weak points in organizational processes and relationships affecting performance and possibilities of improvement)

(11) **Acting as a sounding-board**
(listening to the client's ideas, intentions and plans, giving an expert opinion)

(12) **Providing moral support and counsel**
(listening to people's concerns and complaints, explaining what can be done, providing encouragement, developing an optimistic vision of the future, energizing people)

---

will involve costly developmental work, but once the systems are available it is easy to purchase and apply them, using junior and less experienced consulting staff since the principal job has not been done in the "front room" (where the client is received and served), but in the "back room" (the firm's laboratory and design facility). The client may even be able to purchase the system and introduce it without further consultant help, as a standard medicine purchased from a pharmacy.

**The consultant's principal
intervention techniques**

Clients often ask what exactly the consultant would do in applying the various models and approaches described in the previous sections. Like business executives and administrators, seasoned consultants normally use a wide range of intervention techniques in transmitting know-how and experience to clients and helping them to cope with changes. Table 1.3 provides a list of 12 generic intervention techniques used by consultants in various combinations and variations, and often under different names, in most consulting projects. This list is not exhaustive. Each technique involves the use of a number of other techniques and behaviours, and each technique can be tuned and adapted to facilitate the client's participation. This gives the client and the consultant a rich panoply of intervention techniques for any situation.

1.3. The market for management consulting services

Consultants and clients meet, select each other and negotiate the terms of their transactions at the market for consulting services. The difficulty is of course that there is no centralized market-place, no exchange under one roof where consultants and clients could get together. There are thousands of individual sellers and buyers, all engaged in "retail" trade in consulting through a wide range of marketing channels and techniques: even the world's largest suppliers and users of consulting are directly involved in numerous tiny assignments while simultaneously negotiating or executing some quite important projects.

The market for management consulting services is liberal and open. Choices are free and prices are not controlled. Entry is easy: with rare exceptions (e.g. Austria) there is no need for any diploma, licence, certificate or authorization to start practising consulting. The initial investment can be very small. There are no mandatory conditions, procedures and techniques for carrying out consulting. Legislation must of course be respected, but it would only stipulate the general conditions and rules under which services can be provided against payment.

The consulting industry is self-regulated to some extent by voluntary professional associations. However, this self-regulation only concerns certain aspects of consulting such as the qualifications of consultants and professional standards. Furthermore, consultants who are not members of associations are free to define and apply their own standards.

International market perspective

The largest and most developed management consulting market is in the United States, the country with the oldest tradition in consulting and the most experienced and diversified consulting profession. In 1990 the annual volume of management consulting services in the United States attained some US$ 13-14 billion, generated by over 100,000 consultants. How does this compare with other professional services? In the United States there are some 730,000 lawyers, the American Institute of Certified Public Accountants has 300,000 members and the annual spending on medical care attains US$ 600 billion. Compared with these figures even the American consulting market does not look so large...

The European consulting market can be estimated at some US$ 6-8 billion, with the largest country markets in Germany and the United Kingdom. Central and eastern Europe is the challenge of the future to both the recently established and rapidly growing local consulting firms and the international consulting profession. Estimates from Japan indicate some US$ 2.2 billion, while the rest of the world stays below US$ 2 billion. The total world market was estimated at some US$ 23 billion in 1990.[3]

In the last 20 years growth has been impressive. Despite fluctuations in general business trends, year after year consulting has been able to grow by some 10-20 per cent in a number of countries. This reflects both the interest of business circles in consultants' expertise and advice, and the profession's drive in keeping abreast of changes in the world business environment, diversifying services and marketing them to clients.

Who uses consultants?

The growth and diversification of the consulting market have been fuelled by rapidly expanding and changing demand. Traditionally, private manufacturing firms used to be the principal clients of consultants, in particular as long as consulting was practised mainly in the fields of industrial engineering, company organization and finance. Significant recent changes on the demand side have included:

o   a major shift to the service sectors, reflecting the growth and changing structure of the service economy (banks, insurance companies, health services, travel agencies, leisure industry, social services, etc.);

o   a growing use of consulting services by governments and public sector corporations and agencies (assignments assisting in privatization, structural adjustment, investment projects, performance improvement programmes and more generally in the search for better quality, higher efficiency and utilization of private sector experience in public services);

o considerable increase in the use of consultants by small and medium-sized businesses and even by individual entrepreneurs involved in new business start-ups (through subsidised consulting in certain cases).

Another significant change on the demand side has been the clients' increased sophistication and selectivity in using consultants. More and more clients are able to define with considerable precision the specialist expertise they are looking for, make a careful choice among several candidates, collaborate actively with the consultant who wins the contract and evaluate the benefits obtained. Many clients, especially larger corporations, have established internal consulting and management services which they can use instead of external experts, in collaboration with them or for defining and controlling the work given to outside professionals.

Main types of consulting firm

Professional reputation and solid relations with important clients are the principal assets in the hands of the suppliers of consulting services. Repeat business, i.e. new work for old clients, accounts for 75-85 per cent of the total volume of services in some well-established firms. Thus, once the leading international accounting and auditing firms decided to move into consulting in the 1960s, it did not take them long to become the most important suppliers of consulting services, in addition to their dominant position in auditing, accounting and tax advice. The "Big Six" accounting firms (see Appendix 3) are also among the ten world's largest management consulting firms. The concentration of the business in the hands of large firms, or groupings of firms, is relatively high in consulting – in 1990, the revenue of the 40 largest firms exceeded 60 per cent of the entire world market.[4]

Most large consulting firms have their origin and base in the United States, while only a few of them have roots and headquarters in the United Kingdom or continental Europe. All of them operate as international professional service businesses, with offices, subsidiaries or associated companies in many countries. Most of them provide a wide range of services in all or several areas of management. As a rule, they are able to combine general management services to clients whose problems are broad and vaguely defined and may concern several areas of management, with specialized services in precisely defined functional and technical areas. In addition, they have developed and aimed to maintain a particular technical profile, such as information technology in the case of Andersen Consulting, technology management in Arthur D. Little, strategy and organization in McKinsey, business strategy and restructuring in Roland Berger or job evaluation and remuneration in the Hay Group. Some larger consultancies have chosen to specialize sectorally in health, banking, insurance, telecommunications, chemical industries and the like. Important, but highly specialized firms exist in the areas of employee compensation and benefits, and information technology. The largest international consulting firms are listed in Appendix 3.

At the opposite end of the spectrum, management consulting services are offered by thousands of small firms (two to ten consultants) and solo practitioners. The range of their profiles is extremely wide, but the following characteristics seem to be common to many of them:

o   they are either generalists or specialists;

o   if they are generalists, they work mainly for smaller and medium-sized enterprises in geographically limited areas, maintaining a personalized relationship with the owner or general manager;

o   if they are specialists, they aim to have a distinct product that is in demand and offer a special service in which both small and large clients are interested (a training/consulting package for better time management, organization of maintenance in textiles, improving efficiency of sales agents, etc.);

o   many of them are seasoned, all-round consultants who cherish independence and do not want to be absorbed by larger consulting firms;

o   this group includes professors, authors of management books, retired executives or senior civil servants who have some special knowledge and know-how to sell and may be in great demand even by large and sophisticated clients;

o   this group also includes (unfortunately) a certain number of imposters who have little to offer and would not be employed by a larger professional firm, but who are able to sell their services to poorly informed and credulous clients.

Medium-sized consulting firms, typically employing between 15 and 50 professionals, are spread over the middle of the spectrum. They are of many sorts. Some are traditional consulting practices, which started and continue to work as generalists advising on a wide range of company organization and performance problems for a well-established and faithful clientele. If they identify a need for a specialist intervention and do not employ such specialists on their staff, they would recommend the use of another firm, or subcontract the intervention to a specialist with the client's agreement.

Other medium-sized consultancies have chosen to sell specialist expertise in distinct areas of management, such as maintenance, logistics, project management or sectoral expertise. They look for a "niche" and usually find one by developing and marketing a unique highly specialized service.

Structural change in
the consulting sector

The structure of the supply side of consulting is constantly changing. Although they often advise governments and businesses on structural adjustment, consulting firms have not escaped extensive restructuring themselves in order to adjust to changing demand and growing competition. There have been many mergers of consultancies in the last ten years. Large firms have acquired medium-sized firms because of their specialist skills (e.g. in information technology or corporate strategy), to gain access to markets in other countries or just to grow bigger and stronger than their competitors.

Spectacular restructuring has taken place within the "Big Eight" group of accounting and consulting firms, which shrank to the "Big Six" in 1989 as a result of mergers of Ernst and Whinney with Arthur Young, and Touche Ross with Deloitte Haskings and Sells. Other merger attempts, such as one involving Arthur Andersen and Price Waterhouse, have aborted, but informed observers are warning that the "merger mania" may not be over.[5]

Medium-sized consulting firms have started forming international business alliances to be able to face competition from large consultancies and deal with issues requiring knowledge of the business environment and contacts in several countries.

Further structural changes in the international management consulting industry may be forthcoming. It appears that polarization is taking place, as a result of which many large firms will become even larger, while the small operators will be able to find enough work for which the large consultancies are unsuited, or are too costly. Medium-sized firms will face difficulties in maintaining identity, defining and defending their market niche, and competing with large firms in terms of offerings and quality, and with small firms in flexibility and price. Yet observers of the consulting industry believe that thanks to their adaptability and creativity, the best medium-sized "niche operators" will always have useful services to offer, and enough clients.

Competition in consulting

Although demand for consulting services has grown rapidly and dramatic changes in the global business environment are creating tremendous new opportunities for professional service firms, the market for consulting services has been highly competitive. Consultants compete for clients, and against other consultants, in many ways, but the following are the most important:

o   by aiming to acquire and preserve an image of a highly professional, competent and reliable professional service firm;

- o   by being the first who offers a service in a new area of interest to clients;

- o   by widening the range of services to cater for clients' needs in different areas and subjects;

- o   by building up a rapport of confidence and long-term collaborative relationship with current clients;

- o   by marketing services actively, which includes soliciting new clients and advertising;

- o   by competing across national borders and turning into global professional service firms.

Clients have drawn significant benefits from this competition. They can be more selective and more demanding in searching for the best expertise and the most reliable service, adjusted to their specific needs and requirements. However, fast growth, tough competition and aggressive marketing have also had some negative impact on professional standards. There are firms that have been unable to maintain high standards or have deliberately chosen to sacrifice standards to growth and short-term profitability. Clients have to be aware of these problems, and we shall therefore return to them in the final section of this chapter.

1.4. Management consulting and the world of the professions

At this point it may be useful to broaden our perspective, for management consulting is only one of the wide range of professional services that are available to decision-makers in private businesses and the public sector. As shown in figure 1.3, in a developed economy the professional service infrastructure includes a number of other sectors in addition to management consulting. Auditors, business lawyers, investment bankers and others are often recruited together with management consultants to deal with various aspects of a complex business problem, transaction or project. In other instances, different professional services may compete with each other, in particular if the problem is multidisciplinary, and the client has alternative choices in deciding whether the lead should be taken by a management consultant, an accounting firm, an investment banker or another professional firm.

A detailed description of professional services as shown in figure 1.3 would exceed the scope of this publication. Yet we find it necessary to give a short overview and comment on their changing roles and relationships.

Figure 1.3. The international professional service infrastructure

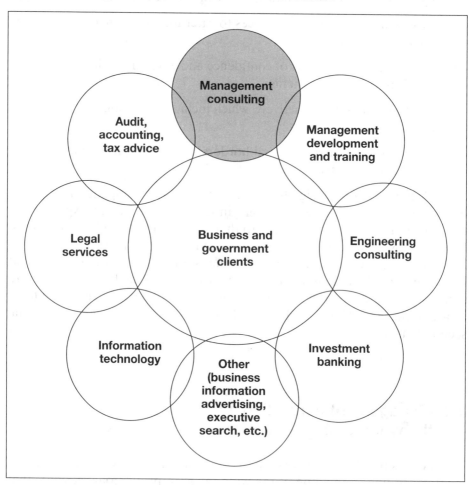

Auditors, accountants and tax advisers

A wide range of professional management services is provided by independent accountants working as sole practitioners or in public accounting firms.

Acting as independent auditors, accountants examine and verify company financial statements (such as balance sheets and income statements) as presented by management and render expert opinion (also called accountant's opinion) as to their fairness, reliability and conformity with generally accepted accounting standards. They refrain from expressing opinion on the quality of management and the possibility of improving it. Normally the auditor's report is short and is issued in a written form. It can be unqualified or qualified. In the latter case, there will be an uncertainty that prevents the auditor from forming an unqualified opinion, or the auditor's opinion will differ from the view presented by management in financial statements. In addition to statutory audits prescribed by legislation and/or company statutes, accountants may be engaged for various other audits whenever management or another party wishes to obtain an independent opinion on a financial or management issue.

Accountants also provide advice and assistance to management on many questions of accounting and reporting procedures, systems and techniques, taxation, financial planning and management, sources of capital and credit, dealing with banks, and so on. The scope and form of this advice or assistance are agreed between the accountant and the client and are not fixed by official regulations. Some accountants perform the bookkeeping and accounting function for business clients, e.g. for smaller firms that cannot afford a full-time accountant. An accountant performing an audit may also be able to form an expert opinion on the weaknesses of management and give other useful practical advice on what to improve, although this is not in the auditor's terms of reference. Tax advice has developed into a specialized service, provided by separate departments in some accounting firms, or by independent tax advisers.

The distinction between the auditing function and providing advice on how to improve accounting and management (and, possibly, even performing accounting operations for the client) is significant since different duties, interests and liabilities are involved, and may be called into question with far-reaching consequences. While accounting and management advice is essentially a private service to management (which retains the discretion to act or not to act on this advice), auditing is primarily a service to investors, lenders and, in a sense, the public at large. Independent and objective auditing is regarded as essential for the functioning of financial and stock markets.

An accountant who has done extensive work for a client on financial policy and management questions may be unable or even unwilling to produce an unbiased and disinterested audit of financial statements reflecting his own expertise and advice. Therefore, some countries insist on keeping auditing and other accounting work strictly separate and have legislation that bars auditors from doing other accounting and consulting work for their audit clients. In contrast, in most Anglo-Saxon and other countries, providing management advisory and other services to clients in addition to auditing is regarded as perfectly correct and efficient by both the legislators and the organizations of the accounting profession.

The synergy effect in doing both audits and other professional work for the same client is obvious. Auditing not only identifies weaknesses and opportunities for accounting and consulting work, but establishes a rapport with the client and makes it easier to market new services to him. Consulting done for an audit client provides the auditor with invaluable knowledge of the client's business, helping to avoid erroneous judgement and wrong conclusions when attesting the fairness of financial reports.

The leading international accounting firms moved into management consulting in the early 1960s and are currently earning a considerable part of their income from management consulting, information technology, systems design, mergers and acquisitions, and other non-audit services. Many other accounting firms have followed the same path.

Investment bankers

Investment bankers are firms whose principal traditional function has been to serve as intermediaries between issuers of securities and the investment public. In the underwriting business, investment bankers, acting individually or as members of underwriting groups or syndicates, purchase new issues of securities and distribute them to investors, either directly or through brokers and dealers. They make profit on the underwriting spread, i.e. the difference between the price paid to the issuing corporation or government agency, and the public offer price. In addition to their basic investment banking functions, most investment bankers also run broker-dealer operations and offer a wide range of financial and advisory services, including services that can also be obtained from accounting, consulting or other professional service firms.

Robert Kuhn groups investment banking activities under 12 categories:[6]

○ public offers of debt and equity securities (the foundation of investment banking, i.e. underwriting);

○ public trading of debt and equity securities (broker-dealer and related services);

○ private placement of debt and equity securities;

○ mergers and acquisitions, and similar operations (including leveraged buy-outs, joint ventures, capital restructuring and recapitalization of companies, and reorganization of bankrupt and troubled companies);

○ merchant banking (where investment banks commit and risk their own capital and seek very high returns; this definition of merchant banking comes from the United States, while in Europe merchant banks are financial institutions that engage in investment banking, the negotiation of mergers and acquisitions, and a number of other financial and portfolio management practices);

○ financial consulting and fairness opinions (on mergers and acquisitions, capital restructuring and similar operations);

o   asset monetarization and securitization (converting illiquid assets, such as small consumer receivables);

o   risk management (hedging against fluctuations in foreign exchange using swaps, options and other techniques);

o   investment research and security analysis;

o   international investment banking;

o   money management (for clients such as pension funds);

o   venture capital (high-risk and high-return investment in young fast-growing companies, often in new and high-technology business sectors).

For example, one investment bank describes its main services for clients in Central and Eastern Europe in the following terms:

o   advice on and assistance with financial structuring (through debt or equity securities) for the public sector, private businesses and individual large-scale projects; placement of these securities with banks and large investors or on the open capital market;

o   advice to businesses and governmental organizations on privatization, corporate structure, company valuation and mergers, particularly with western industrial partners;

o   advice to Western companies on acquisitions in central and eastern European countries, and on structuring and placement of the necessary equity and debt capital.

Mergers, acquisitions and similar major business and investment deals may involve, in varying proportions, the services of management consultants, accountants and auditors, business lawyers and investment bankers. Thus, any of these professional service firms can act as a finder, i.e. a person or an organization that introduces two parties to each other, possibly helping them to exchange information and start negotiating a deal, with the expectation of a fee. For company valuation, the client might consider using a management consultant, an accounting firm, an investment banker or even another professional firm.

In cases where alternative choices apply, it will be important for the client to be aware of the strengths, weaknesses and possible biases of each sort of professional service firm. For example, assessing potential future earnings of a manufacturing company requires an excellent knowledge of demand and sectoral trends, maturity level of the technologies used, emerging technologies, local competitors, existing and potential foreign competitors, factors affecting the prices of principal inputs and the like. Accountants and investment bankers normally do not possess this information, but can obtain it through management consulting and business research firms.

Legal services

Legal advice is required in connection with many business and management decisions. The demand for legal advice has increased in line with recent economic and social developments such as:

○   the growing complexity and new forms of business deals and transactions, in both national and international business, commerce and finance;

○   the introduction of new legislation affecting various aspects of business, employment and industrial relations, in areas such as the environment, quality standards, consumer protection, insurance, liability, rights of minorities or equal employment rights;

○   the progression of regional economic groupings, such as the European Communities (EC), which involves the development of common legislation in substantive law concerning such areas as free movement of persons, goods and services, banking, insurance and other financial services, taxation, competition, dumping, technical standards or product liability;

○   major structural adjustment and economic reform programmes involving various forms of privatization, company and capital restructuring, stock and financial market organizations, and even total revision of the legislation regulating business, commercial and financial operations, taxation, employment and industrial relations;

○   individual citizens and companies turning increasingly to litigation in resolving conflicts in certain countries.

Numbers of organizations, especially the larger ones, employ in-house lawyers, who may be able to handle a great deal of the legal work required. For example, over 400 lawyers are employed by General Electric and more than 250 by General Motors. Even large corporations turn to independent law firms in cases that are reserved to independent lawyers by legislation, or when particular expertise is unavailable in the corporation. Independent law firms range from sole practitioners through medium-sized generalist or specialized firms to large firms employing over 1,000 lawyers (this, however, is considerably less than the number of professionals employed by large firms in accounting and management consulting).

While the markets for legal services have been expanding steadily and reputable firms could not complain about a shortage of work, in competitive markets, such as the United States, lawyers have been looking for new ways of improving their competitive advantage and rendering new services to clients. Law firms have started specializing in services such as legal advice to financial institutions, bankruptcy, environmental law, space law or even sunken treasury law. Specialization is increasing within traditional areas such as corporate law, and clients want to be served by lawyers who are recognized experts in precisely defined areas of legal practice.

A recent change has been the legal firms' branching out into non-traditional services, including those that are outside the scope of the legal profession. This has included consulting and counselling services to clients in business management and economics, finance, environmental protection, real estate, engineering, psychology and others.

The idea of full service or one-stop shopping has thus found its way to the legal profession. If a country's legislation or the code of conduct of the profession prevent lawyers from providing such a service within the firm alongside legal services, or if non-legal professionals cannot become partners of the law firm, alternative organizational formulas are sought, such as working through subsidiaries and sister companies. In the United States, this formula was pioneered by the Washington-based law firm Arnold and Porter, which established three subsidiary firms for non-legal services in general-purpose consulting, consulting to non-profit organizations and services to banks and savings institutions.

A parallel development has been the expansion of legal services to clients by accounting, management consulting, investment banking and other professional firms. As a rule, these services are provided as part of a wider service package, e.g. in preparing and negotiating a merger or acquisition involving firms in two or more different countries.

Instances of collaboration between professional firms in law and other sectors are also common. The initiative often comes from the legal side: a lawyer may identify the need for management, accounting or financial advice in dealing with a legal problem, and turn to a management consulting or accounting firm, which may or may not already be on contract to a common client. Conversely, it may be the management consulting or accounting firm that perceives the need for legal advice and suggests that the client should seek consultation with internal counsel or recommends that the client should engage outside counsel, either directly, or through a subcontract issued by the consulting or accounting firm.

Information technology consultants

Over the past two decades, information technology (IT) has become a critical factor of competitiveness and success in all areas of business. The speed with which hardware and software have been changing, and the number of new applications, has been staggering. This has required considerable capital investment and growing operational spending on information processing.

Despite increases in the number of information systems and computer specialists employed in companies, managers have also been increasingly interested in ad hoc and short-term special services concerning various aspects of information technology selection and use. A new area of professional and support services to management has emerged that started operating as an essential link between the producers and the users of commercial hardware and software.

According to data provided by the Computer Service Association in the United Kingdom, the Association's member services to clients are in the following main areas: software products (14 per cent); custom software specifically designed for individual clients (16 per cent); total systems/systems integration (20.4 per cent); consultancy (16 per cent); education and training (3 per cent); data processing (6 per cent); database services (4 per cent); facilities management (7.3 per cent); recruitment and provision of contract staff (6.3 per cent); and third party maintenance (2.5 per cent).

Consultancy, accounting and other professional service firms from various backgrounds have moved into IT services. At the present time, all important accounting and management consulting firms treat IT as a priority growth area in their service portfolio. Their focus is on management applications, systems design tailored to specific management needs, adaptations of standard software packages, equipment selection and systems integration.

Computer service companies represent a second group. Their services include systems design and programming, education and training, network development and management, telecommunications, and systems integration.

A third group includes computer equipment manufacturers and producers of commercial software. Their involvement in IT services and consulting is of more recent date, but has progressed rapidly and is likely to grow.

In all these cases it is often difficult to determine what IT services should be categorized as management consulting. The limits of management and IT consulting are increasingly blurred. Furthermore, management and IT services tend to be ever better integrated and offered to clients as parts of one service package. While associations of management and computer consultants are separate organizations in several countries, the cases of the BDU in Germany or the SYNTEC in France are worth mentioning since they link management and computer consultants in one intersectoral professional federation.

Engineering consultants

The terms "engineering consultants" or "consulting engineers" are used generically to cover persons and organizations intervening in a consultant capacity in areas such as civil engineering, architecture, the construction industry, land and quantity surveying, transportation, urban and country planning, project design, planning, supervision and evaluation, mechanical, electrical and chemical engineering, patent services, technology transfer and so on. Even management consultants used to be called consulting engineers in the early years of consultancy.

A common characteristic of consulting engineers is that they are qualified professionals in private practice. Therefore clients can turn to them for independent counsel and assistance, as well as in seeking special help in areas where they are short of expertise. This includes independent and objective advice on contract preparation and negotiation, as well as on the selection of contractors and suppliers of equipment and materials.

Management consultants and consulting engineers may collaborate or compete in areas such as project planning, organization and management, production engineering, planning and control, plant design, factory layout, materials handling, maintenance management, quality management, productivity improvement or feasibility studies. In some instances the client has the possibility to choose between management consultants with engineering and production background, and consulting engineers versed in organizational and economic aspects of production and other processes.

Executive search consultants

Executive search (head-hunting) has developed as a special field of consultancy in response to an ever-growing demand for executive and specialist talent, combined with a shortage of qualified individuals and recruitment difficulties in key areas of competency. The service is offered by executive search firms, or by specialized units within larger multi-functional consulting and professional service firms. In the latter case, executive search can be performed as a separate assignment, or as part of a wider service package concerned with company restructuring and reorganization, or human resource management.

Businesses turn to executive search specialists if they do not want to advertise a job publicly, if they seek candidates in areas where advertising does not normally work and, in particular, if they feel that an executive search firm has a better chance of locating the best candidate owing to its knowledge of the sector and sources of talent, information base, and methods used for locating and screening candidates. An executive search firm does not operate as a general employment agency, but as a focused service, knowledgeable about the industry or service sector served, recruitment, interviewing and assessment techniques, organizations where candidates can be located, and the ways in which offers have to be made and negotiated in order to attract qualified candidates.

Executive search firms aim to develop in-depth knowledge of the market for high-level managerial and specialist talent in particular sectors (e.g. transport), functional areas (financial management) or both. They operate impressive databases on potential candidates and also use advertising. The leading firms are international, or cooperate with other firms to be able to serve international clients and locate candidates in other countries. A new service added to their portfolio by several leading firms is the identification and provision of temporary executives.

As executive search has to comply with local labour and employment legislation in every country, various practices are used. There are, however, certain common rules and principles, such as strict confidentiality, the rule that the fee is paid by the client company and never by the candidate presented, or the principle that search is undertaken exclusively at a client's request. Some executive search firms have expanded their services into various aspects of human resource management, development and compensation.

Management development and training services

Finally, one sector of professional management services is probably closer to management consulting than any other service. We have in mind management development and training provided either as an internal service within the organizations where managers are employed, or externally by a wide range of institutions and organizations, private and public, including many consulting firms. The general purpose of management development is to increase managerial competence and effectiveness by improving the managers' knowledge, attitudes and skills, and helping to apply in practice what the managers have learned in various training and development events.

The relationship between management consulting and management development has many facets which ought to be kept in mind in selecting and using consultants. Let us point out the most important ones.

The first facet was mentioned in section 1.1. If the client participates actively in the consulting assignment and if the consultant works in a way that enables and encourages the client's learning, consulting also plays the role of managerial and human resource development. People learn and develop by working with consultants on new tasks and acquiring their consultant's diagnostic, interpersonal, organizational and change-agent skills.

Secondly, management consulting and management development can supplement and support each other in pursuing specific objectives in improving management competence and organizational performance. In addition to identifying and solving problems, the consultant's work also identifies needs and suggest suitable approaches to developing managers and employees. Changes proposed by consultants, such as new management techniques and systems, may require considerable management and staff training, which may be provided directly by the consultants as part of an assignment, or by specialized training and development services, internal or external. Conversely, training and development generate needs and specific requests for consulting.

If a manager decides to apply what he has heard and appreciated in a course, he may turn to a consultant with a request for practical advice.

Thirdly, in certain cases the client can choose between consulting and training. He may turn to a consultant with a request to help in finding a solution of a specific problem, such as introducing more appropriate and productive scheduling and control systems. Or the production manager and his specialist staff may attend a course on production planning and control and then prepare and introduce the required changes without calling any consultant.

These close relationships and the possibilities of making alternative choices have influenced the profiles and intervention methods of both consulting firms and management development institutes and centres.

As regards consulting firms, they have always used management training and development as one of their intervention techniques combined with other techniques in executing particular assignments. More recently, many consulting firms have started offering training programmes that are not necessarily linked to one particular assignment, but aim to provide information, skills and know-how reflecting the consulting firm's general experience gained through a number of assignments. Some consulting firms offer open training and development programmes in addition to tailor-made or bespoke programmes that are designed and mounted for specific clients. Quite a few consulting firms operate management centres and institutes offering a wide range of courses, seminars and workshops.

Turning to management centres and institutes, including university-level institutes and business schools, their involvement in consulting, and the sort of consulting services they are able to provide, differ from case to case. Some of them have established full-time consulting services operated by special consulting departments. In most institutes, however, consulting is a part-time activity in which faculty members engage in addition to delivering a certain amount of training through courses and seminars. As a rule, their consulting is quite individualized, i.e. faculty members negotiate and carry out the assignments individually and in small teams in areas of their technical competence. Most of these assignments would be of smaller size, e.g. advice on policy or strategy issues, but seldom a comprehensive diagnosis, restructuring or turnaround of an important company, a task for which most management institutes would lack resources. Many assignments are in the area of human resource management and development and include the design and delivery of in-company training programmes adapted to the company's specific problems and needs.

A client considering whether to use management teachers and trainers as consultants should be able to establish whether they are merely looking for some practical experience and additional income, or are able to provide special knowledge or practical expertise that are not available from consulting firms or are offered by management consultants under less interesting terms.

Options available to large and small business clients

Certain lessons can be drawn from our review of particular sectors of professional services.

Clearly, the world of professional services has changed quite considerably in the last ten years and will continue to change. Hence, the first conclusion – if you want to be a well-informed user, you cannot view these services as they were ten years ago, but must keep informed about their trends and changes to be able to tap up-to-date expertise in the most efficient way.

The traditional borders between professions have become blurred. Lawyers are in management consulting and tax advice, accountants in mergers, acquisitions and legal advice, management consultants in education and training, computer firms in management consulting, and so on. There are two main reasons for this: competition and the client's interest in integrated services.

Competition is an important driving force affecting the structure and behaviour of professional service firms. They compete for clients and markets with other firms within the same profession (accountants with other accountants) and with other professions (management consultants with computer firms). Thus, several accounting firms and investment bankers have decided to offer legal advice to clients rather than sending them to independent law firms.

Thanks to these developments, in most countries clients enjoy considerable possibilities of choosing among professional service firms offering various arrangements and conditions. In Chapters 3 and 4 we shall see that technical proposals and price quotations can be requested from several professional firms and then negotiated with one or two firms whose offers look most interesting both technically and financially.

The client also has several options in deciding with how many partners to deal in handling various aspects of a complex project or transaction.

It can make a lot of sense to clients if they can seek and obtain financial and technical services supplemented by and coordinated with advice on various aspects of the problem at hand (managerial, fiscal, legal, technological, etc.) from one source rather being referred to a number of separate sources of information and advice. Some clients prefer to purchase services that have been selected, co-ordinated and packaged for them by one service firm rather than going through lengthy selection, negotiation and co-ordination in dealing with several firms separately. In such a case the client may be able to obtain an integrated service portfolio directly from one larger firm or agency; or one firm (e.g. a management consultant) may be chosen as leader and co-ordinator, with the mandate to identify and present to the client suitable professional firms for specific professional tasks (legal advice, search for partners, engineering, etc.). The client may then use these firms as subcontractors to the lead firm, or recruit them directly. These are merely examples, since large business and government clients use and coordinate professional services in many different ways.

Turning to small business clients, their problem is that they need nearly the same range and diversity of professional advice on various aspects of the business as large firms, but normally this advice will be simpler and should be provided in ways that make it easily accessible and "user-friendly" from the viewpoint of small entrepreneurs.

If you are a small business client, and if you can afford it, you can of course decide to deal directly with various independent professional advisers – a management or business consultant, a lawyer, an accountant, a tax adviser and so on. Many small business people prefer to call on organizations, private or public, able to provide an integrated service package virtually under one roof (one-stop or one-window service). There are many different types of such organizations. As a rule, they can combine general business consulting with training, information and specialist advice on questions such as marketing, quality, credit or taxes, and also help to find and negotiate credit and obtain the necessary loan guarantees.

1.5. Professional standards

If there is one distinctive feature that characterizes consulting and other professional services and underlines their difference from other goods and services, it is neither technical expertise nor the art of providing advice to clients, but professional integrity. Professional services can exist as such and play their role in economic and social life if the principle of integrity and ethical standards permeates all their activities, opinions, statements, and relations with clients. Whenever this principle is forgotten or sacrificed to the commercial interests of the consultants, the service provided can no longer be called independent, objective and professional.

The role of professional associations

Over the years, the professions have established various types of bodies to define and defend their common interests and promote professional standards. In management consulting, the first national association, the Association of Management Consulting Firms (ACME) in the United States, was established in 1926. At the present time such associations can be found in all countries where the consulting sector has attained some importance (see

Appendix 1). There are countries where consulting firms are organized in one association, while individual consultants as persons can be members of another association (called "institute" in some countries with an Anglo-Saxon tradition). The main functions of consulting associations include:

○ acting as guardians of qualifications standards (by defining and applying membership criteria that require the applicant to demonstrate and prove necessary knowledge and a record of practical achievement); in some countries the consultants' institutes practise certification on a voluntary basis and members meeting certain criteria of competence, experience and professional conduct can become certified management consultants;

○ defining and promoting a code of ethics and professional conduct (in applying for membership, consultants agree to adhere to the association's code of ethics; there is, furthermore, a control and disciplinary procedure that may lead to exclusion of members who have acted against the code);

○ promoting the profession with the clients (through information services, directories, advice on consultant selection etc. – as discussed in Chapter 3);

○ providing services of common interest to members (training seminars, information bulletins, workshops and publications on professional firm management, etc.).

Membership of consulting associations is voluntary and on average about half of the consultants practising in a country are organized in these associations. There are consultants who do not qualify for membership (e.g. they do not meet the association's qualification standards or practise consulting as a part-time or occasional activity) or do not find it interesting to engage in association work and pay membership fees. Most of the important consulting firms are members, but there have been some significant exceptions (some of the leading consulting firms feel that they do not need the associations).

Codes of ethics

It would be an unfortunate misunderstanding if a client expected the consultant to apply rules and standards that are not practised in a profession and are not supported by a code of ethics. Therefore it is essential to know what is regarded as professional conduct by the organizations of the profession. Such information can be easily obtained from consultants' associations – all of them have adopted codes of ethics or professional conduct and are happy to communicate their codes to their members' current or potential clients. The associations' officers would always answer questions concerning interpretation of the code. Moveover, you may ask your consultant for a copy of the code adopted by his firm. Even if the firm is not a member of an association, it should be in a position to communicate and discuss its own code of conduct and enclose it with the contract you are going to sign.

We can also recommend that you ask for any clarification of particular clauses of the code that look unclear or incomplete to you. Consultants are used to answering such questions before signing contracts or during assignments and will be happy to speak about their ethical and behavioural norms.

Let us now look at several important professional standards applied in consulting.

Avoiding misrepresentation

The first condition of behaving as a professional and respecting the client's interest is giving true and correct information on the consulting firm. Clients should be able to examine this information in detail and ask for more information if they are not satisfied. Consultants are bound to inform clients correctly:

○   on the firm's competencies and the sort of work it can undertake (this is very important in restructuring economies and developing countries, where some clients are not able to ask the right questions in examining the consultant's background and capabilities);

○   on the sort of work performed for former clients (referrals provided with the former clients' permission);

○   on the consultant's ability and readiness to assign staff of the right competence to the assignment;

○   on the time span within which the job will be completed if both the consultant and the client respect their commitments.

Being objective and impartial

As mentioned in section 1.1, the client's interest can be served if the consultant maintains full objectivity and impartiality throughout the assignment. As a client, you do not want to face someone who always agrees with you, but a professional who would always give an independent opinion even if this differs from what you would like to hear, and risks irritating you. Impartiality means that the consultant must not get involved in the client organization's internal politics. It also requires considerable self-control on the part of the consultant, in particular in dealing with people of different nationalities, cultures, religions or political profiles, so that his technical service does not become tainted by emotions or prejudices.

Disclosing information on commissions received or paid

As a general principle, professional consultants and advisers should not pay or accept any commissions in order to be chosen for assignments or for providing services and favours somehow related to the given assignment. Yet commissions and discounts are practised, and in some countries constitute an inevitable way of obtaining and doing business. The codes of conduct of professional associations tend to be incomplete and ambiguous about this question. At best they ban accepting commissions, but are conspicuously silent about paying commissions.

Paying a commission to a potential client's employee in order to influence the consultant selection process, or to a current client's employee in order to get the consultant's report accepted or contract extended, is nothing else than bribery. However, a consultant or another professional may pay a commission or extend a favour to another person who introduced him to a new client.

It is impossible to provide universal guidance on what commissions are acceptable from the viewpoint of professional ethics. Local business practices and cultures are an important environmental factor that are difficult to ignore. As a general rule, the client should be made aware of commissions and similar favours received, paid or promised by the consultant in connection with the assignment. Omitting to disclose commissions or promises of commissions about which the client should be informed is unprofessional.

Respecting confidentiality

Without confidentiality there could be no consulting. If you are using a professional adviser it goes without saying that he will neither disclose any confidential information about your organization nor make use of such information to obtain any benefits. While the general rule is crystal clear, there may be difficulties in its practical interpretation:

o   What information is confidential and should be treated as such? If you sense any risk of misinterpretation on the consultant's side, brief him fully about your conception of confidentiality.

o   All consultants use experience from past assignments when working with current clients. It will be the same in your case. For example, an analysis of your specific financial ratios will help your consultant to become more knowledgeable about management and financial practices of firms in your sector. However, the consultant must not disclose your specific ratios without your permission if you regard them as confidential data.

o   You may not wish your consultant to have access to your firm's confidential information that is not directly related to the assignment. You should discuss this early enough with the consultant and your staff to avoid any misunderstanding.

o   A specific system designed and developed by the consultant for your company should not be transferred to other companies unless you agree with the consultant on the conditions of such transfer.

Charging a fair fee

We have explained that professional firms are businesses that have to compete in the market and pursue commercial objectives alongside professional standards and objectives. This fact is reflected in the relationships between the real value of the professional service rendered to the client and the price paid for this service. It is difficult to compare the product of consulting services with other products, and the consultant may be the only person to know how much time and effort was really required to complete the assignment. Therefore a fair fee is very much a question of ethics. The consulting profession regards as unethical:

o   failure to inform the client in advance about fee levels and billing practices;

o   to take advantage of the client's ignorance and charge an excessive fee, or undercut fees and work at a loss in order to win a new client (knowing that sooner or later the fee will have to be increased to the normal level);

o   to accept an assignment whose cost is out of proportion to the limited benefits likely to be obtained by the client.

Avoiding conflict of interest

Conflict of interest is perhaps the most important and delicate ethical issue in professional services at the present time, when both client firms and their professional advisers are complex organizations involved in a wide and steadily changing range of activities guided by various interests, which are often difficult to identify, assess and analyse. Conflict of interest may be created not by bad faith and malpractice, but by ignorance and the failure to give it due consideration on either the consultant's or the client's side.

Questions of conflict of interest tend to become increasingly complicated and blurred in using large multifunctional consulting and other professional firms, and the services of investment bankers. Therefore, in working with various advisers on complex transactions such as mergers, capital restructuring, turnarounds or major investment projects, clients should ask their consultants about any activities, relationships, interests and commitments that might be in conflict with the client's interests. Because uninformed clients are not always able to ask all questions pertinent to the danger of a conflict of interests, it might be better to ask the consultant in general terms, inviting him to inform the client about any existing or potential conflicts of interest. If the client forgets or does not know how to ask, the consultant should himself take the initiative and inform the client of any possible conflicts.

A few examples may illustrate what conflict of interest means in professional services:

o The consultant is a director or has ownership or other interests in a firm that is trying to acquire your firm or has accepted an assignment that is related to this acquisition. The conflict of interest is blatant.

o The consultant will provide advice on the selection of equipment or systems, but is directly or indirectly associated with, or will receive a commission from, a supplier of equipment or computer software. There is no conflict of interest if the client is informed about this relationship and the financial stake involved, and if he agrees to purchase a package including advice, selection and equipment and system delivery. There is conflict if the client is not informed.

o The consultant is simultaneously, or within a short time, employed by two or more competing firms in the same sector, e.g. automotive industry. This occurs frequently when using sectorally specialized consultants who obviously cannot avoid working for competing clients. Avoiding conflict of interest is a delicate issue, but the leading professional firms are well aware of it and have developed various safeguards to protect each client's interests and avoid undesirable information leaks. In certain cases they even turn down assignments to be sure that they do not lose their clients' confidence due to conflict of interests.

o The consultant is recommending another branch of his multiservice professional firm to the client for a job for which another firm would be more competent or offer a better price. This occurs quite frequently, although the conflict of interest is obvious.

o The consultant tries to recruit your staff for his firm or another client instead of helping you in staff development. The conflict of interest is obvious and such practices are banned by the consultants' code of ethics.

o The consultant is proceeding with the assignment and sending his bills although he is clearly on a wrong track, nothing will be achieved and the client's money will be wasted. The conflict of interest is blatant.

Consultant and client ethics

To be fair, we have to look at the other side of the coin as well. Consultants can proceed and behave in accordance with the profession's ethical norms if they have clients whose attitudes and dealings also comply with basic ethical norms. It would be unrealistic to expect the consultant to strictly apply high ethical standards in working for a client firm involved in fraudulent dealings. A professional consultant who finds out that he risks becoming entangled in such a situation would normally draw the client's attention to his finding and, if there is no change, withdraw immediately from the assignment.

In other cases, clients may request services that the consultant is not prepared to extend, such as giving a favourable expert opinion on a transaction or project that the consultant is unable to endorse, or conveying confidential information that the consultant acquired in previous assignments with other clients.

Often it is impossible or impractical to refer the issue to higher management, a professional association or an independent authority. The consultant and the client should discuss the issue frankly and find a solution, or terminate their relationship.

The client's role and responsibility in promoting professional standards in consulting and other professional services cannot be overemphasized. If you want consultants to observe and exhibit high professional standards, you should not ask any single member of the consulting, accounting or any other profession to ignore these standards because it suits your selfish commercial interests.

The limits of professionalism

A word of caution is necessary at the end of this chapter. We have described the many excellent services that clients can obtain from professional consulting, accounting, legal and other firms. We have placed considerable emphasis on professional standards, and on the consultants' and clients' roles in ensuring the application of these standards.

The growth of professional services has followed, and in certain cases even anticipated the expansion of national and international businesses and the ever-growing demand for special expertise and know-how in vitally important areas and aspects of management and business. On the whole, consulting and other professional service firms have been able to meet their clients' changing demands and provide services of satisfactory quality. Yet it would be unwise to trust every professional blindly and accept his advice or expert opinion without any scrutiny. Clients ought to be aware of cases of professional negligence and even malpractice that have occurred in various professions, and which even some of the largest and highly reputable professional firms have not escaped. The reasons are seen in the extremely fast growth of the professions, the recruitment of large numbers of people by these firms who start working for clients without sufficient training, instruction and guidance by experienced consultants, the numerous mergers and acquisitions of professional practices, and the shift of focus from technical proficiency to profitability and salesmanship. In commenting on recent changes in the accounting profession, Stevens points out pertinently that for generations members of the leading firms considered themselves as "professionals who happened to be in business". In the 1980s, this view was reversed and since then they see themselves as "business people who happen to be professionals."[7]

All in all, professionalism has limits. As a user of consulting and other professional services you ought to be aware of these limits. This will help you to avoid misunderstandings and failures, and maximize the return on resources spent on using consultants and other professionals.

---

[1] Milan Kubr (ed.): *Management consulting: A guide to the profession* (Geneva, ILO, 2nd (revised) ed.,1986); pp. 13-17.

[2] See Miles H. Overholf and William J. Altier: "Participative process consulting: The hard and soft of it", in *Journal of Management Consulting*, Vol. 4, No. 3, 1988, pp. 13-23.

[3] The data are from *Consultants News*, June 1991, and other sources.

[4] *Consultants News*, June 1991, p. 3.

[5] Cf. Mark Stevens: *The Big Six: The selling out of America's top accounting firms* (New York, Simon and Schuster, 1991).

[6] See Robert L. Kuhn: *Investment banking* (New York, Harper and Row, 1990).

[7] Stevens, op. cit., p. 22.

ON DECIDING THAT YOU NEED A CONSULTANT

2

Problem-solving is a basic characteristic and component of the management process: managers spend most of their time and energy on identifying and analysing problems, and trying to find solutions that work. Most management problems are identified and handled by everyday routine activity of managerial and specialist staff. As soon as one problem has been successfully handled, another problem emerges and has to be addressed, and so it goes.

There is, however, a class of problems that escape routine handling and tend to become a matter of concern. Managers are reluctant to tackle them and often do not really know how to proceed. The problem may be repeatedly mentioned in board and management meetings, but nothing is decided. In other cases, everybody feels that something is wrong in the organization, but when asked to be more specific people talk about quite different things.

There may be many reasons underlying these problems: their novelty, vagueness, complexity, rapidly changing nature and scope, the range of conflicting interests involved, the far-reaching impact on the future of the business, and similar reasons. A public enterprise that has never been exposed to private business practices has to come up with a privatization programme involving a foreign partner. A marketing manager who has never worked with Asia is told that he may stand a good chance in several Asian markets if he takes quick action. Or there may be a feeling among managers that their firm's market position will be seriously affected when a rival firm launches its new product on the market, but no one is able to suggest what to do about it.

These are examples of problems that are potential candidates for consulting assignments. Under certain circumstances, it may be more effective to recruit a consultant to help management tackle such a problem, rather than spending time and energy in searching for a solution that is apparently beyond the company's capabilities, or delaying the solution of the problem until there is a crisis.

What, however, are these circumstances? How can one identify problems that are important enough and justify the cost of a consultancy? What should management do before deciding to call a consultant? At what stage of problem diagnosis should a consultant be brought in?

In this chapter, we shall try to answer these questions. Section 2.1 focuses on problem identification by the client in preparing for a consulting assignment. Section 2.2 reviews a number of criteria whereby a client would normally judge whether he should use a consultant in solving company problems. Finally, Section 2.3 discusses how a client defines and describes the terms of an assignment before selecting a consultant.

True enough, some managers do not bother identifying their problems and the pros and cons of using a consultant: they feel that the consultant can do this for them. Alternatively, a manager's decision to use a consultant may be emotional. The manager was impressed by the breadth of his knowledge and his professional approach in a management seminar, or the consultant has visited the company a few times and the manager has had interesting discussions with him; now he feels that he has actually made a commitment and cannot say no to the consultant's offer to do some work for him. This, however, is not a typical managerial stance in initiating consulting projects. Managers have to be pragmatic. If a manager gives serious consideration to using a consultant, he normally wants to be sure that this decision will be fully justified and supported within the company, that the right consultant will be chosen and that the company will draw clearly spelled-out benefits from the assignment.

2.1. Problem identification

In a rational approach to the use of consultants, clients start by identifying and defining their problems. Accordingly, we shall first explain what we mean by "problem" and discuss issues involved in problem identification.

Problems in general

The term "problem" is used in all areas and sectors of human activity. It is a generic term, a label, that can mean almost anything, and we often use it as a matter of convenience if we do not want to be, or cannot be, more precise. Figure 2.1 shows the results of one particular exercise where a group of people were asked to indicate the connotations which the word "problem" had for them. Ten different connotations were identified, but the reader could easily add others.

Any situation can be viewed as a problem if there is a difference or discrepancy between what is (or will be) actually happening and what should (or might) be happening. Therefore a problem can only be described in relative terms, as a difference between two situations; a situation *per se* cannot be a problem. It is also important to see that subjective judgement is always

Figure 2.1. Some connotations of the label "problem"

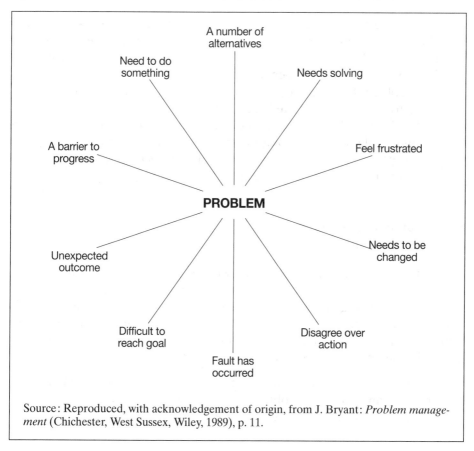

A number of
alternatives

Need to do
something

Needs solving

A barrier to
progress

Feel frustrated

PROBLEM

Unexpected
outcome

Needs to be
changed

Difficult to
reach goal

Disagree over
action

Fault has
occurred

Source: Reproduced, with acknowledgement of origin, from J. Bryant: *Problem management* (Chichester, West Sussex, Wiley, 1989), p. 11.

involved – a situation or a relationship is perceived as a problem only if someone believes that it should be different from what it really is.

A person's attitude to a problem, and interest in having the problem solved, is fundamental. If a lorry is parked in front of your garage and blocks the path, it is not a problem. It becomes a problem once you have decided that you want to get your car out of the garage and have found out that the lorry is locked and the driver absent. You have compared two situations and concluded that one of them is inconvenient to you. It will be your problem, not your neighbour's or other people's problem.

The same applies to problems in management and business. A problem for one company is a joy to its competitors. Within the same organization, a problem which has made the marketing manager lose sleep may be of no concern to the accounting department – unless it is established that the problem will significantly affect global business results and the interests of people outside the marketing sector, including those working in accounting.

Problem ownership

This brings us to the concept of problem ownership, which is very popular in literature on problem-solving and consulting. Every problem has one or more "owners". These are the people who are affected by the existence of the problem and will draw some benefit from its resolution. They regard a situation as a problem because they would like it to be different. Therefore they are likely to be more interested than other people in having the problem resolved and will probably be prepared to make a greater effort than others in finding and implementing a solution appropriate from their point of view. Conversely, they may resent it if someone else starts tinkering with "their" problem without asking for their views and participation.

Signals of management and business problems

The initial signal of a problem may come from anywhere in the organization or from the outside. The process starts with the realization that something is or might be going wrong, or not as well as in other companies. At this point it may be only a feeling – an impression – reflecting experience or intuition, or management may already possess precise and detailed data showing inadequate performance or trends that threaten the company's future.

Five groups of signals warrant management's attention in identifying management and business problems. These five groups are complementary rather than exclusive, and overlap to some extent.

Information on undesirable performance and trends

A number of indicators signalling existing and latent problems are shown in table 2.1. This information will be available from activity and performance records, management and accounting reports, audits, special surveys and other sources. Most signals in this first group will be quantified and it will be relatively easy to make comparisons which will give a first idea about the magnitude of the problem.

Signs of malaise in the organization

Quite different from the previous group of signals are feelings of dissatisfaction, tension, fatigue, loss of perspective and other signals of poor working climate, worsened interpersonal relations and generalized malaise. Although it may be difficult to make them explicit and various people will perceive them quite differently, these signals usually reflect the existence of human and organizational problems.

Table 2.1. Signals of undesirable trends

Indicator	Situation
Output	Low/falling
Standards of service	Low/falling
Scrap/waste	High/rising
Standards of human performance	Low/falling
Time taken to perform tasks	Long/rising
Level of accuracy	Low/falling
Use of equipment	Low/falling
Accident rate	High/rising
Labour turnover	High/rising
Absenteeism and tardiness	High/rising
Recruitment problems	Continuing/increasing
Labour disputes	Excessive/increasing
Market share	Low/shrinking
Delays in delivery	Excessive/increasing
Customer complaints	Excessive/increasing
Growth rate	Low/diminishing
Profitability	Low/falling

New opportunities and threats

A third group of signals conveys information on developments that will either create new opportunities or constitute threats and risks for the company's future development. They point out changes in the business and social environment concerning markets and competition, government policies and legislation, environmental and health protection standards, availability and prices of raw materials and energy, developments in the labour market, technologies, sources and methods of finance, structural adjustment trends and processes, and so on. In this area, information will be either quantitative (e.g. growing prices of inputs) or qualitative (e.g. a conservative government has won elections, with likely changes in legislation). Most of these signals will concern various aspects of the external environment and to identify them management will need to screen a wide range of information sources.

Behaviour of other companies and managers

The behaviour of other companies and managers is a most useful source of information and inspiration. By comparing your behaviour with that of the sectoral leaders and other companies known for their excellence and dynamism, you will be able to gain insight on what might be changed in your company. This information might be obtained directly from business contacts and friends, through industry associations, from business and professional journals and other mass-media information, and so on.

Suggestions from consultants and other professionals

Consulting and accounting firms, and management schools and institutes, as well as individual researchers, professors and writers, are a prolific source of ideas and offer an ever-growing range of proposals for improving management and increasing efficiency. You can receive their suggestions through individual contacts, in workshops and conferences, from books and articles and so on. An examination of their ideas, descriptions of work performed and specific services offered may uncover various problems and opportunities in your organization.

A closer look at these five groups of signals reveals one very important thing. There are signals which will be available in every organization where record-keeping and management attains minimum quality standards: unless it is totally mismanaged, any company will collect and analyse information on customer complaints or staff turnover and absenteeism.

Conversely, there is a wide range of information that is not readily available within companies and may be quite difficult to obtain. Information on various environmental trends, new technologies, foreign markets, financial systems, legislation under preparation or innovative programmes of management institutes may be systematically collected and analysed by companies of a certain size and sophistication, but it is beyond the possibilities of most small and medium-sized companies to deal with it regularly and systematically. Two solutions are available to these companies: turning to secondary information sources, such as specialized information agencies and journals, or using the services of consulting firms with distinct expertise in collecting and analysing environmental and similar information for their clients.

Analysing the problem

When it comes to problem analysis, normal practice in an organization will be to distil the "special" problems that may justify the recruitment of a consultant from the vast amount of routine signals, symptoms, difficulties and problems identified by management or brought to its attention everyday on a virtually permanent basis. This requires problem analysis which, at this stage, will be preliminary and quick, the purpose being not to solve the problem entirely but to define it more precisely and decide how it should be handled.

In analysing a problem, the client will be looking for the characteristics listed in table 2.2.

It could be objected that the characteristics mentioned under (1) to (5) in the table define the problem without doing anything about it, while those listed under (6) to (9) imply that problem-solving has started. In management practice, problem-solving does not consist of separate stages that can be strictly isolated from each other. In signalling a problem, people are likely to suggest a cause and even a solution. There is nothing wrong about this. Such information can be very valuable and ought to be properly recorded and examined. It would of course be wrong to endorse these first remarks on potential causes and solutions without further testing, as this might reduce, right at the beginning, the chance of finding the real cause and the appropriate solution.

There is, then, the question of how far to pursue this preliminary problem analysis. A pragmatic approach is the best one. If the problem-solving process has made a good start, people have become enthusiastic and there is obviously a desire and capability to go ahead, it may be counterproductive to impose an artificial barrier and stop the process. The problem will be diagnosed and resolved without a consultant although the original objective of the analysis was to justify a consultancy. Management may, of course, have reasons for not letting the process continue spontaneously. Limited resources and the need to assign priorities may be a valid reason: if people become enthusiastically engaged in the solution of the problem, they will not be able to deal with another problem, which may be more important and more urgent.

Table 2.2. Characteristics of a problem

(1)	Problem substance or identity (lack of new ideas, obsolete technology, loss of important market, etc., keeping in mind the difference between problem substance and symptoms).
(2)	Location (division, workshop, building, etc.).
(3)	"Ownership" and awareness (people directly affected and interested in having the problem resolved; Who is aware of the problem?).
(4)	Importance (to unit and/or whole organization, also in comparison to other problems).
(5)	Time perspective (urgency, when first detected, recurrency, former attempts to resolve the problem).
(6)	Causes (factors and forces that have created the problem).
(7)	Influences (forces that may facilitate or hamper problem solution, relationship to other problems).
(8)	Ideas on possible solutions (often people submit these ideas spontaneously along with the statement of the problem).
(9)	Benefits to be drawn from the solution (quantified and qualitative, such as increased motivation or an improved working climate).

Common errors in problem identification

Errors in defining problems limit the possibility of solving them. Unfortunately, some errors are quite frequent, and therefore it is worth reviewing them at this point.

Mistaking symptoms for problems

This is probably the most common error. A condition or relationship is described as a problem, although it is only an effect. A reluctance to take risks and innovate may be stated as a problem, but it may be a symptom of other problems, such as lack of management support to initiative and innovation.

Preconceived ideas about problem causes

There may be the tendency to see the same causes behind all problems, such as lack of motivation, poor training, government interference, and so on.

Identifying problem causes from a position of power

This is a variant of the previous case. The views of an individual in a position of authority are accepted as an unqualified definition of the real causes.

Failure to discern cause and effect

This may happen if conditions influence each other, and it is difficult to determine the real cause. This is the so-called vicious circle. Is low work morale a cause and poor work quality and insufficient output an effect, or vice versa? Or is there another cause?

Unfinished problem diagnosis

In diagnosing business and management problems, we face chains of problems and causes. The issue is how far and how deep to go in searching for basic (primary) problem causes. If diagnosis stops too early, the principal cause will not be identified and addressed.

Failure to examine various aspects of the problem

This happens easily if there is a tendency to view all problems as structural, financial or human, and to ignore or play down other aspects of multidisciplinary problems.

Failure to examine how the problem is perceived
by various parts of the organization

Organizational processes typically cut across various functions, units and teams. Ignoring these relationships leads to distorted and biased problem analysis.

Again and again, these and similar errors are made even by experienced decision-makers and trained problem analysts. One reason lies in the very nature of business and management problems, which are difficult to grasp and define due to their complexity, multidisciplinary nature and the fact that in practical business life it is virtually impossible to separate one problem from other problems and influences. Another reason is vested interest. Because problems exist only if people perceive and define certain situations as problems, it may happen that the key persons involved do not wish the problem to be defined, or present a biased definition. Often the decision-maker – the principal owner of the problem – is too close to it and so emotionally involved that he is unable to determine and acknowledge the real nature and dimension of the problem. His own attitudes and behaviour may be the main problem, and if this problem cannot be addressed, any other problem-solving effort will be futile.

Closed-ended and open-ended problems

Problems can be looked at and classified from many different perspectives, but the following classification has been found practical and useful by many consultants.

A closed-ended (or "tame") problem is one whose causes can be relatively easily identified and removed if logical problem-analysis and problem-solving techniques and the right technical expertise are correctly applied. The problem can be isolated from environmental forces and described fairly accurately. Once it has been identified, it is possible to devise an action plan or a project to find and apply an appropriate solution.

In management, closed-ended problems are those that can be resolved by distinct changes in systems and techniques such as replacing one operations scheduling and control system by a more advanced and efficient one.

An open-ended (or "wicked") problem is different because it is influenced by many factors, its causes are less easy to identify and describe, there may be a wide range of solutions and it is not possible to determine the limits of the problem in terms of time, ramifications, units, people involved, and so on. Often many aspects of the problem cannot be seen and addressed before some progress has been made in solving the problem.

There are two broad classes of open-ended problem. The first includes general problems of business policy, strategy and performance. Poor business and financial results may be the key symptoms of these problems, but the causes can be numerous, including those that are not under the company's control, and some rapidly changing causes. Alternatively, the company's current performance is judged as satisfactory, but there is a feeling that the company is capable of performing much better in the future.

The second class of open-ended problems includes those which are predominantly human and behavioural. They are characterized by tensions, clashes, breakdowns in communication, reluctance to cooperate, gossip and other symptoms of a poor working climate. People tend to be emotional about these problems and their symptoms. Individual and group behaviour will almost certainly be affected by conflicting interests.

In management and business, many problem situations exhibit characteristics of all these groups simultaneously: general business and financial difficulties are interwoven with human and behavioural problems, while certain aspects of the total situation can be handled by distinct changes in techniques and systems.

Problem analysis should aim to identify to which of these groups the problem at hand belongs, or what its predominant characteristics are if it belongs to more than one group. We shall see that this is essential for determining the nature of the consultant's expertise and method of intervention.

Who does the analysis ?

The designation of persons responsible for problem identification and analysis in preparing for consulting assignments reflects management's feelings about the complexity of these problems, and about people's ability and willingness to define them correctly. If there is a work organization problem in the sales division, but the sales manager is not made responsible for defining the problem and the requirements for a consultancy, this is a signal of lack of confidence, or of clumsy decision-making, insensitive to people's concerns and susceptibilities (which is not infrequent in bureaucracies).

Ideally, if the problem owner is known or can be identified, he should be made responsible for this task. His mandate should be to define the problem as precisely as possible and justify why a consultant is necessary. If the problem owner is short of time, staff or technical expertise, a formula can be found to help him by providing support from specialists such as internal consultants, systems analysts or training officers. A task force can be established, problem identification workshops organized, and so on.

If the problem appears to be complex and important enough to the business as a whole, general management should take the lead and do the analysis with the support of its closest collaborators. This does not preclude consultations and the use of committees or task forces to clarify the problem and collect ideas on possible solutions. However, if a potentially significant problem is totally referred to committees or junior staff, this is likely to be perceived as a lack of senior management's interest, and a preconceived value judgement about the low importance of the problem.

2.2. Why use a consultant?

Problem identification produces data and generates ideas needed to address the second question, namely if the problem requires the recruitment of a consultant. In this section, we shall successively examine the main factors that will be considered in making this decision.

Is the problem important enough?

Bringing in a consultant is not a routine management action, and during the consultant's presence in the organization business will not be "as usual". The assignment will be a special project and if your organization is in difficulties, the consultant's intervention may be close to a course of medical treatment at a doctor's surgery. Time, effort, understanding and intellectual input of your people will be required.

It would make little sense to refer all problems that look difficult to consultants. It is essential to select problems that are important enough, judged not merely by their size but their impact on your organization's objectives, operations and results.

Therefore management's approach should be pro-active: not to wait for ideas and requests coming from various parts of the organization (with more or less solid justification), but to detect key problems, with significant potential impact, in priority areas of top management concern and corporate strategy. To achieve synergy and higher impact, priority will often be given to choosing problems that are related to each other rather than embarking on a number of isolated problems in different areas of company activity.

This does not mean that closed-ended problems in narrowly defined areas could not be important enough and eligible for consulting assignments. For example, the problem may concern the organization of workshop maintenance services. Many consultants are recruited for their distinct specialist expertise in areas such as maintenance, operations scheduling and control, or quality management. Here again, the same basic considerations will apply. Is the problem just puzzling someone in the organization or will its solution have significant impact on the quality of our products and services, productivity and financial results?

Since any organization has limited human and financial resources for handling several consulting projects simultaneously, problems have to be compared in terms of their relative importance. If the maintenance manager requests three assignments, but cannot handle more than one within the next 12 months, which one will be selected? Frequently, the number of requests exceeds the company's possibilities and management is charged with the delicate task of severe screening.

Is the timing right?

Correct timing is essential. Often a consultant is brought in when it is too late and is only able to find out that the problem cannot be solved any more. There will be a crisis, but it is too late to prevent it.

This can be avoided by assessing the degree of problem urgency and making sure that problems rated as both important and urgent are handled with priority. Consultants in turn are sensitive to the issue of urgency. They will be prepared to review your assessment of problem urgency with you and discuss arrangements whereby work on urgent problems starts without delay, even if it means changing work schedules concerning less urgent problems.

Sometimes a proposal concerning a problem that is not seen as urgent is submitted either within the company by a functional manager or internal auditor, or comes as an unsolicited proposal from an external consultant. The client may be exposed to some pressure to accept the proposal if the consultant stresses that he now has time but will be very busy in a few weeks. Here again, the company's priorities and possibilities will provide the main criterion for judging unsolicited proposals. If the proposal passes the test, because it addresses a significant problem and comes from a competent consultant, management may choose to consider it favourably (see also Chapter 3 on consultant selection).

Are you sure that you cannot handle the problem?

The lack of competence, or expertise, is the main reason for using consultants in problem-solving and managing organizational change. At some point of the problem-identification exercise described in the previous section, the client will have a sufficiently clear and complete picture of what needs to be done, and the desired results, to consider if the organization is short of relevant competence for handling the problem.

"Shortage of relevant competence" can have many different meanings. It is not a negative value judgement, a statement of incompetence. The typical situations in recruiting consultants will be:

o total lack of staff for certain technical tasks (the consultant will provide the expertise that is lacking);

o competent staff are available but are too busy doing other things (the consultant will provide more of existing expertise);

o the problem is open-ended and highly complex, and the client wants to supplement his own diagnostic and change management expertise by external information, insights and know-how;

o in the area concerned by the assignment the client has standard sectoral expertise, but lacks special, more advanced knowledge or know-how and is not able to develop them in a short time, or their development would be too costly.

Current management problems to which these criteria apply are often in the area of computerized information systems. Management identifies the problem quite precisely – for example, slow response to customer orders despite high volumes of stock of finished products and work in progress due to an archaic information processing system in marketing and manufacturing. The solution should be a new system for receiving and processing orders, scheduling and controlling operations and dispatch, and handling exceptions. However, the design and introduction of such a system is an important specialist task, for which the company's small computing department would need more than two years without being able to guarantee optimal selection and full utilization of state-of-the-art hardware, systems and know-how. Therefore the client concludes that the most effective approach is to recruit an information systems consultant who will develop and install the new system according to specifications prepared by the client, and under the client's supervision.

Do you need help in diagnosing the problem?

There are situations where the client finds out that he could not progress and get far enough in initial problem identification. This may be due to various reasons. Either the situation of the whole business is too complex and difficult and is influenced by a wide range of external and internal forces, or the general atmosphere is poisoned, loaded by emotions and conflicts, people are troubled and unhappy, but no one is able to suggest how to get any closer to understanding the causes and start dealing with the real cause. It is quite typical of organizations in difficulties that they cannot do much about their problems because they do not even see them. In other cases, the client is just short of the time and resources to identify the problem and describe it correctly.

If this is the case, it is justified to bring in a consultant at an earlier stage – not on the basis of completed problem identification, but in order to help the client with it. This implies that the consultant will be faced with a very preliminary and often vague statement of the problem as perceived by the client, and will have a mandate to carry out the diagnosis together with the client or on his behalf.

Many consultants prefer this approach since it helps them to gain a better insight into what is really going on in the client organization, establishes a collaborative relationship at an early stage of the process, before the client has made up his mind about the nature and importance of the problem, and reduces the risk of disagreement between the consultant and the client about the definition of the problem and the objectives of the assignments.

It should be stressed here that even if the consultant does not participate in problem identification and is presented with detailed terms of reference describing the project, he will rarely be prepared to accept the client's statement of the problem at face value without verifying whether the client has not misunderstood the problem and misinterpreted the situation. Many consultants have burned their fingers by accepting mandates based on incomplete or biased problem identification. One of the basic rules of consulting, reflecting many years of experience, tells the consultant to check whether he can subscribe to the client's description of the problem and the mandate given to the consultant. Consultants do this in various ways, such as quick verification of the problem description in preparing an assignment proposal. However, most of them regard collaboration with the client in the preliminary problem identification as the most useful way.

Will benefits exceed costs ?

When preparatory work has progressed enough and the scope of the assignment has become clearer, it will be possible to give consideration to the benefits that the assignment should produce and their comparison with the necessary costs. Here again, the client will have to decide if he has enough information and experience to produce and compare reasonably accurate figures, or if he needs a consultant's assistance in this exercise. In comparing future financial benefits with current costs, the client will use one of the discounted cash flow analysis techniques.

Both quantitative and qualitative benefits will be considered. Since improved business results and performance are the bottom line, an attempt will be made to assign values to qualitative results. For example, what increase in sales can be expected if the assignment will improve the morale of salespeople? Figures that are obviously wrong or based on wishful thinking will, of course, be discarded even if presented as data resulting from serious analysis. If problems ought to be tackled whose results are essentially qualitative (work morale, motivation, interpersonal relations, teamwork), the client will refer mainly to experience and judgement in determining how much such improvements will be worth to the organization.

Are resources available?

Even if the project's effectiveness is unquestionable, the client organization must be able to mobilize finance to pay the consultant and defray other costs to be incurred, and allocate necessary staff and management time.

The staff time and its cost must not be underestimated. Clients frequently make the mistake of authorising resources for consulting fees, but taking no measures to allocate staff time. This is a major cause of inefficiency in consulting since the consultant, despite the high cost of his time, cannot proceed with the job as scheduled. Also, the client misses numerous learning opportunities.

Will you overcome psychological barriers?

For some managers the decision to use a consultant will be psychologically difficult. They will be loath to admit that an outside expert could be able to understand and improve anything in their company or department. What can a consultant achieve if our best people, with years of experience in the sector and an intimate knowledge of organizational culture and policies, have tried and failed?

A manager may start worrying about his personal image or reputation. The decision to bring in a consultant might be interpreted as a recognition of personal weakness and even incompetence. If a company turns to a consultant, its customers and other business contacts might be alerted, thinking that the company is in trouble. Managers might be under fire from both sides – they risk being criticized from above, e.g. by the board of directors or by a supervisory body in the public sector, for not having acted earlier and not having tried to make improvements without relying on an expert from outside. From below, there can be open criticism of management or hidden irony ("you see, these people have been telling us what to do and now they need a trouble-shooter").

Even if there is no such criticism, and if the use of a consultant is generally perceived as a sound management decision aimed to make a strong company even stronger, the decision-maker may have to swallow a bitter pill. His pride and ego may be affected, especially if the consultancy will have to touch on behavioural issues, interpersonal relations, personal work style and other delicate questions.

Should you decide against using a consultant?

If the arguments produced and the assessment made are inconclusive, your decision on the use of a consultant will be negative, or you will decide to restrict or postpone the project. As already mentioned, it is good management practice to insist on thorough justification, especially if people are coming to you with many different ideas and you definitely will not be able to act on all of them.

In its guidelines to clients, the ACME in the United States suggests the following four rules:

o   Do not hire a management consultant until you have tried to develop a clear understanding of the project objectives.

o   Do not hire a management consultant unless you have full commitment from management to support the project financially and organizationally.

o   Do not hire a management consultant to run your business indefinitely. A management consultant has a professional responsibility to see that the recommendations are implemented, but it is your responsibility to decide how to implement them and with whom.

o   Do not hire a management consultant unless you are prepared to provide ongoing support during and after the project. Many assignments require client personnel to be retrained and to supervise the programme after implementation to ensure its success.

2.3. What sort of consulting assignment?

If the basic decision on the use of a consultant is positive and due consideration has been given to the points reviewed in the previous sections, the client will have enough material to define the consultant's task. At this point it can be assumed that many discussions have taken place, many ideas have been put forward, and people will have various views on what has been actually agreed and what questions have remained open.

To avoid ambiguity and unproductive speculation, it will be useful to summarize in writing all conclusions reached, as well as supporting information. This will force people to be specific and disciplined in finalizing their thinking and will avoid fuzzy definitions and ideas. Alternatively, this step will reveal that only vague and very preliminary conclusions could be reached.

A document in which the scope of a future assignment is outlined is called the terms of reference (TOR). Other frequently used terms are job specification, work specification or statement of work.

Terms of reference

It is useful to produce the first draft terms of reference as soon as possible. You will thus obtain a basic statement that can be reviewed, discussed and modified within your organization in order to reach consensus on what the consultancy will be about. You may decide to limit the use of a consultant to a range of tasks for which you lack information and competence. Therefore, the consultant will deal only with a part of the problem identified in your preliminary study. The drafting, circulation and discussion of the terms of reference should make this clear, thus signalling to your staff that other tasks remain their responsibility and will not involve any consultant.

The terms of reference are the initial statement of the work to be undertaken by a consultant. They may be fairly precise and detailed, and may include a lot of background and supporting information, if you have gone a long way in preparing for the consultancy and if your diagnosis has been thorough and detailed. In contrast, they may be summarized in one sentence if you can present a broad statement of your problem but expect the consultant to carry out a detailed diagnosis to check your definition of the problem and make it more specific before proposing any action.

The terms of reference tell the consultant what to do. Yet a rigid interpretation of this role would be counterproductive. Unless you are absolutely certain that your initial statement of the problem is correct and complete, the terms of reference must be regarded as an open-ended statement that can be completed and revised at a later stage in the assignment.

If a selection procedure is used, as will be discussed in Chapter 4, the terms of reference will be distributed to a number of potential candidates who may not be familiar with your organization. Therefore the TOR will have to provide background information and data in addition to the statement of the consultant's task. Confidentiality ought to be kept in mind, however.

The checklist in Table 2.3 shows what is normally included in the terms of reference. The pitfalls to avoid include:

○ nebulous terms of reference, reflecting feelings and wishes rather than solid investigation and problem definition. In such a case, the message given will lack clarity and precision. The consultant will be unable to make a sensible proposal, or the terms of reference will lend themselves to various interpretations and the proposals received from consultants will not be comparable and will actually describe quite different assignments;

○ excessively detailed terms of reference, implying that you know the solution and the consultant cannot do anything other than copy the terms when preparing the proposal. The purpose of the selection procedure and possibly of the whole consultancy will be missed. The proposal you will get will actually restate your problem in the consultant's terminology. It will contribute little to the diagnosis of the problem and you will receive hardly any useful ideas from the consultant on how to approach the project. Your very decision to turn to a consultant may be questionable: since you know and can tell in detail what is to be done, why use a consultant?

Table 2.3. Terms of reference – Checklist

- Description of the problem(s) to be solved.
- Objectives and expected results of the assignment (what is to be achieved, final product).
- Background and supporting information (on client organization, other related projects and consultancies, past efforts to solve the problems, etc.).
- Budget estimate or resource limit.
- Timetable (starting and completion dates, key stages and control dates).
- Interim and final reporting (dates, form, to whom, etc.).
- Inputs to be provided by the client (further information and documentation, staff time, secretarial support, transport, etc.).
- Exclusions from the assignment (what will not be its object).
- Constraints and other factors likely to affect the project.
- Contact persons and addresses.

Scope and nature of the consultant's intervention

The terms of reference will reflect your thinking about the required scope and focus of the assignment. In large and complex organizations, any project can lead to other projects and it may be difficult to decide when the product is final if this has not been clarified at the beginning. The choices to be made will concern organizational units, processes, products, categories of personnel, alternatives to be explored and other aspects. For example, in seeking a foreign partner for a merger, you may decide to limit the search to potential partners of a certain technical profile and volume of business, and from selected countries.

Your most important decision will concern the nature of the envisaged intervention. Based on the nature and scope of the problem, the resources that your firm can allocate and the context in which you are planning to start the assignment, you will determine what exactly you want the consultant to do and what intervention methods you want him to apply. In this way you will also define the profile of the consulting firm you will be looking for.

If your problem is closed-ended and largely technical and has been well diagnosed, you will be planning a specialist intervention and looking for technical experts in the area of the assignment – maintenance management, production engineering, vehicle fleet management, quality control, production of customized software for operations scheduling, sales force training, and so forth. The consultant may have to do a major part of the work, with as much participation of your staff as possible, however.

Complex business strategy and general management problems will require a different type of intervention and consultant profile. The scope and course of the assignment is likely to be defined in less detail and with less precision. The diagnosis of the business will probably have to be pursued in considerable depth and a number of alternatives may have to be explored. Knowledge of sectoral trends, main technologies, markets, competitors, potential partners, sources of finance and similar will be essential. You will be looking for a consulting firm able to take a comprehensive view of your business and think of restructuring and performance improvement opportunities from a broad national and international perspective. High flexibility, the ability to change the focus of the assignment during implementation, and access to additional sources of information and expertise will be required. Yet you will not want the consultant to start doing any work that you would prefer to do yourself with your staff. You will be looking for experts in strategy and restructuring who will not "fix it for you" but who will be prepared and able to work with you because they believe in participative consulting and are able to apply it in practice.

If you sense or have established that human problems dominate the situation and prevent the solution of technical and business problems, the assignment may be focused on issues such as interpersonal relations, team-building, motivation or communication within the organization. You will be looking for a consultant with a behavioural science background and skilled in dealing with organizational behaviour issues in practice. Careful consideration will be given to the question if human and behavioural problems can and should be separated from technical and business problems faced by your organization, or if it is technically justified and tactically more appropriate to deal with these problems simultaneously. Your preference may go to a consultant who intervenes mainly in a process-consulting mode, but who is able to assume other roles and provide specific technical expertise whenever this is required.

Obviously these are just examples of approaches to defining the assignment and the required sort of consultant intervention. They do not exhaust the subject and do not provide any blueprint for all situations, but illustrate the client's considerations in defining the scope and nature of the assignment. The results of these considerations may be fully reflected in the terms of reference, in particular if the assignment will deal with a well-defined and predominantly technical problem. In other cases, the terms will suggest a desired profile of the assignment and the consultant, but further discussions with the consultant will be required to reach understanding on what actually can and ought to be done.

Who will be the client?

Being specific about the client's participation and roles in the assignment helps to define responsibility and make sure that resources will be allocated in all units concerned by the assignment. Moreover, a decision has to be made on a most critical issue in managing and implementing consulting assignments, namely who will be the consultant's client and in what way the consultant will assist the client.

The question may look paradoxical. On the previous pages we have been referring to your organization and your role as manager in defining the need for a consultancy. Is it not obvious that your organization, with its top management, is the client?

From a legal and institutional point of view the consultant-client relationship will be formally established between two organizations that will sign the consulting contract. However, in consulting the term "client" is also used to denominate the persons who will be negotiating and working with the consultant and playing key roles in the assignment.

In a large and complex organization, the consultant will have to deal with many people and touch upon many questions and issues. Therefore some consultants refer to "client systems", taking a systems view of the client organization and trying to map out the network of relationships in which they will operate. Problems arise if these relationships are confused and the roles misunderstood. For example, the consultant was brought in by top management with the understanding that the main client relationship will be with the production manager, in whose sector the assignment will be carried out. However, the marketing manager is also heavily involved due to the influence of marketing practices on production organization and planning, and vice versa. Who will be the main client? How can the top manager intervene during the assignment without taking all the initiative and responsibility away from the production manager? Confidentiality issues are also involved, since even within the same organization the consultant may not reveal all information collected, and all proposals prepared, to all units and individuals without the principal client's agreement.

To clarify the client system issue, Edgar Schein suggests thinking of four categories of clients:

o   contact clients, who approach the consultant initially;

o   intermediate clients, who get involved in early meetings and planning the next steps;

o   primary clients, who own a problem for which help is required;

o   ultimate clients, who may or may not be directly involved with the consultant but whose welfare and interest must be considered in planning and carrying out the intervention.[1]

The "primary" or "principal" client will probably be entrusted with the main responsibility and leading role in preparing, negotiating and implementing the assignment, even if higher management wishes to be kept in the picture, contribute to the project and retain the right to take the key decisions. Probably he has demonstrated enough interest and commitment in the previous steps, in identifying the problem and justifying the need for a consultancy. Therefore it will be only logical if he continues in the primary or principal client's role once the assignment becomes operational.

Of course, one of the conclusions of problem identification might also be that the problem owner cannot or does not want to be the principal client. He may resist the changes that will inevitably result from the assignment, or may be incapable of understanding what is going on and why a consultancy is necessary. If this is the case, the principal client's function should probably not be imposed on him. If the project is regarded as necessary, a higher-level manager may have to assume the principal client's role, or the manager in question may have to be replaced even before the project starts.

---

[1] Edgar Schein: *Process consultation*, Vol. II (Reading, Massachusetts, Addison Wesley, 1987), pp. 117-129.

ON CRITERIA AND METHODS
OF CONSULTANT SELECTION

3

The selection of consultants will be discussed in two chapters. This chapter will deal with the criteria and methods of selection, while in Chapter 4 we shall look at procedures normally used in selection. The general purpose of consultant selection is obvious: you have come to the conclusion that you need a consultant and you want to find and recruit the best one that you can afford. This is fully understandable. An outsider will be looking into your "internal cuisine", dealing with your problems and making recommendations that may affect the future of your firm and possibly even your personal position. Does this not justify the recruitment of the best expert? The difficulty lies in the matching of the consultant's profile, capabilities and availability with the importance and complexity of the job to be done, the culture of your organization and your personal preferences, including, of course, your time, and financial and other constraints.

3.1. What are you selecting?

Selection can be a straightforward process if your problem is highly technical and precisely defined, and if it is in an area where only one or very few technical experts are eligible candidates. This, however, is not typical for most consulting assignments in management. It is almost certain that a number of firms of various profiles, backgrounds and dimensions will be capable of undertaking your assignment. In addition to domestic firms, quite a few foreign firms might be eligible and interested. There may also be professional firms from other sectors that have branched out into management and business consulting and offer services in the area of your assignment.

The fact that you need a consultant implies that you may be approaching selection with feelings of uncertainty and fear, and even some aversion, in particular if you have little experience with choosing and using consultants and suspect that the choice will be a delicate matter. You realize that in buying a professional service you are getting a promise, an expectation, and that uncertainty can be somewhat reduced by careful selection, but there is no way in which it can be completely eliminated. After all, this uncertainty is also due to you: before the assignment starts you cannot say if you yourself and other people in your organization will accept or resent the consultant and how you will work with him.

Although the final product of the consultancy is difficult to define and remains uncertain, you will aim to reduce this uncertainty and increase the chances of getting a satisfying product by selecting:

o   a professional firm known for providing excellent service;

o   individuals on that firm's staff who possess acceptable technical expertise, with whom you will be able to work and whom you will trust in the pursuit of a common goal;

o   a design of the consulting assignment that, according to your and the consultant's judgement, is likely to produce the best results;

o   various logistic, organizational, financial and other conditions which will facilitate the achievement of these objectives.

Let us mention, at the outset, two basic rules for consultant selection. The first rule stresses that the client is selecting the consultant, and not the consultant the client. This is not a tautology. We shall see that consultants influence potential clients through quite sophisticated and dynamic marketing and may take initiative in offering services to specific clients. If this happens to you, you do not have to be suspicious and reject the consultant right away: although unsolicited, the offer may be of real interest. However, you are in charge and your decision should be based on the same selection criteria as in other cases, and not on the fact that the consultant has come to your firm and given some time to you and your people and therefore you feel obliged to say yes.

The second rule concerns the relationship between the complexity and importance of the problem at hand (including the financial stake) and the amount of effort and time spent on search and selection. Selection can be made extremely meticulous, lengthy and time-consuming if you want to be sure that you have investigated all possible alternatives. But is it justified and can you afford it? Is the assignment important enough? The law of diminishing return applies in consultant selection as in any other area of business. Conversely, assignments that are delicate and critical to the future of your business will deserve most careful selection.

3.2. Consultant selection criteria

There are no universal or standard criteria for choosing consultants. Every client is free to define his own criteria, reflecting his company's expectations and experience with the use of consultants. Yet the application of the following eight criteria has helped many clients to appoint the right consultant:

o   professional integrity;

o   professional competence;

o   rapport with the consultant;

o   assignment design;

o   capability to deliver;

o   ability to mobilize further resources;

o   the cost of consulting services;

o   the reputation or image of the consultant.

Professional integrity

Professional integrity is not really a criterion, but a fundamental condition of selection. Many questions will be easily answered and problems avoided if clients never compromise on integrity and ethical standards, as discussed in section 1.5. If you have doubts about any aspect of professional ethics and conduct, and cannot get satisfactory answers, you should not consider using the candidate.

Information on professional conduct of particular consultants circulates in client circles and the issue can be raised with former clients. Standards of professional conduct can be observed or discussed with the consultant during the selection process. The candidate may be able to provide a copy of his firm's statement of professional ethics, and may tell you if it is identical to or different from the standards of the professional association to which the firm belongs.

Certain questions deserve frank discussion. For example, the risks of conflicts of interest on both the consultant's and the client's side should be reviewed. Other questions do not have to be asked directly. The consultant will reveal a great deal by talking about himself and his firm's achievements, clients, competitors, the consulting industry and other subjects.

Professional competence

Professional competence is another criterion that in most cases can be treated as a condition of selection – only candidates who exhibit required competence will be regarded as eligible, and judged by further criteria. This, however, is more easily said than done. The reason is that professional competence is a relatively broad concept, which is less precise and more difficult to grasp than many people may think.

Of course, it is not difficult to obtain and evaluate information on some obvious aspects of technical competence, such as:

o   the consultant's education, degrees, diplomas and further training and development;

o   the length and type of his experience in management and in consulting;

o   references provided by clients for whom he has done comparable work;

o   membership and work done in a professional association or institute (which may have provided the consultant with a diploma as a "certified consultant");

o   books, articles, research papers and other technical documents published by the consultant.

Many clients would decide, on the basis of this information, if they regard the consultant as competent or not. However, if you want to say that you have given full consideration to the issue of competence, a few more questions need to be examined. Five of them are particularly important:

Competence of the firm and the individual consultant

Both of these are to be assessed. In recruiting a firm, you are buying its competence. This will be delivered to you through the operating consultants working at your organization. It is understandable that these consultants' personal competence cannot be equal to the firm's competence. Therefore, how does the firm guide, backstop and supervise its consultants working in field assignments and how does it ensure quality? In this respect, the requirements of different assignments are not the same. If the job consists in developing a system or methodology that the consulting firm has helped to install at other organizations and for which it can provide some standard system or its outline, a junior consultant may be fully competent to do the job under senior consultants' guidance and supervision. Conversely, if the job involves a great deal of judgement, choice and decision-making in a situation that has no precedent, the firm will have to provide a more experienced and versatile consultant, working rather independently from the consulting firm's management but able to draw on its resources when appropriate.

In-depth knowledge of the client's industry

Many consulting firms have made a strategic decision to build expertise and be recognized as experts in specific sectors of industry or services, such as automotive industry, textiles, building and construction, insurance, health or transportation. The client has to consider if the assignment requires excellent knowledge of the sector and practical experience with doing consulting in that sector. This may include understanding of specific business practices, traditions, habits, terminology, managerial and workers' attitudes, industrial relations and other characteristics of the sector, in addition to questions of sector technology and economics. Generally speaking, specific sector expertise may be an advantage in a wide range of assignments concerning business strategy, restructuring, operations and marketing. It may be less essential in finance and human resource management, provided that the consultant is able to learn quickly about sector characteristics and differences from other sectors where he has worked. Sector specialization may imply working for clients who compete with each other; therefore consideration will also be given to potential conflict of interest (as mentioned in section 1.5).

In-depth understanding of the client's country and culture

If consultants from a foreign country are being considered for a job, it will be essential to determine how important the knowledge and understanding of your country is to the success of the assignment. Generally speaking, consultants are aware of the role of environmental factors in providing professional advice and are fairly sensitive to social, political and cultural factors, and to different economic, legal and institutional settings. There is, however, a difference between being generally sensitive to such issues and knowing and understanding them in depth in a particular country environment.

If a consultant should start working in a country that is new to him, it would be unrealistic to expect that he will possess any intimate knowledge of local conditions. However, he must do his homework in preparing for a meeting with a prospective client, and not only when he is sure to win the contract. Furthermore, it is not the client who should pay the whole cost for the consultant to learn about the new environment. Moving to new countries requires research and preparation, and consultants have to invest in this as would any other business company. Conversely, if you are seeking advice from a highly competent expert in a very specialized and possibly narrow technical field, insisting on in-depth knowledge of your country may be unnecessary and counterproductive.

"Hard" and "soft" skills

The term "hard skills" describes the consultant's ability to understand and use procedures, techniques and systems that can be formally structured, quantified and described and relatively easily transferred among people with appropriate educational backgrounds. Hard skills are needed for all areas of consulting but prevail in financial analysis and management, operations and

---

materials management, logistics or computerized information systems. "Soft skills" concern human attitudes, values, feelings, relationships and behavioural patterns. They are needed for understanding and influencing the human side of the enterprise, motivating people, resolving conflicts and managing changes that affect human interests and feelings.

Therefore in choosing a consultant, it is important to consider the relative importance of hard and soft skills for tackling a particular job. The client will then aim to compare the candidate's profile with the profile of the job. The consultant may be an outstanding technical expert in his field, but he may be known for having a difficult personality and poor relations with people. The client will have to consider if he can himself handle the human side of the assignment to avoid personality clashes and resistance to change, in order to be able to make use of the consultant's exceptional technical expertise. Fortunately, consulting has made great progress in balancing hard and soft consulting skills, and cases of outstanding technical experts with poor communication and human relations skills are becoming rare.

Creativity and innovation

It is also useful to ascertain if the assignment requires a great deal of creativity and innovation or if it is a rather routine job, similar to those done by the consultant for previous clients. To many clients the consultant's professional competence is summarized in the classical question: "Have you done it before?" This is a value-laden question and implies that past experience is the best proof of the consultant's ability to tackle your problem. It is useful to ask this question in any event. However, the fact that the consultant has handled a similar job before may not be the right reason for choosing him. If a new and innovative solution is to be sought, the consultant's ability to challenge conventional wisdom, view problems from a wider perspective, use research methods, work with computer models and generate new ideas will be more important than past experience with similar jobs.

Rapport with the consultant

If for any reason you could apply only one criterion of choice, your rapport with the consultant would probably be the safest one. The reason is that this criterion embraces other criteria if you know the consultant reasonably well and if you are yourself a person of sound judgement. Probably you would not have a good rapport with a consultant who is unreliable or technically weak.

Your rapport with the consultant is a relationship between people, not organizations. This point is very important since there is no guarantee that the same rapport will develop between other people assigned to the project by the consultant's and the client's organizations. This rapport is based on trust above all. You trust the consultant's integrity, commitment and judgement. You believe that he is not going to cheat you and take any advantage of your ignorance, absence, distress or shortage of time to control all his movements.

There may be three different situations:

o   You have worked with the consultant and know him from direct personal experience. If this experience has been largely positive or even exceptionally good, this relationship has a great value for you as a prospective client for other assignments. It will simplify choice and reduce the risk of mistakes. For example, you may be unable to judge if your consultant has all the know-how and enough experience to tackle a task that is new both to you and to him. But you will be sure, and feel comfortable, that he will offer to handle only those tasks that really are within his capabilities. Consultants know well how important this relationship of trust is to both the clients and themselves. This is perhaps the main reason why they attach so much importance on repeat business and on maintaining an excellent relationship with existing clients.

o   The second situation is one in which a personal relationship is being established between a client and a new consultant. The two have not collaborated before and do not know each other. The client may even be suspicious and distrustful on account of some not very happy past experience with professional advisers. The consultant has a short time to get to understand the client and to demonstrate his concern, during preliminary contacts, a short diagnostic survey of the client organization or interviews set by the client. During this short time, a rapport will be established and a climate of mutual understanding will develop, or not. Some consultants mention "the first five minutes" during which it already becomes clear whether the consultant and the client can work together. David Maister has identified a number of major concerns of a buyer of professional services (see table 3.1). Since in most cases more than one candidate meets the terms of reference and is judged as equally competent by the client, the consultant's personal characteristics, and his ability to inspire confidence and dissipate the client's worries will become the decisive criterion of selection.

o   In a third case, the personal relationship will be established outside your work context – for example, you meet a consultant at a social gathering or a sports club. You may be impressed by his personality and conclude that to use such a person as an adviser might be a good decision. Indeed, this might be a way of initiating a productive work experience. However, it would be naive to assume that a pleasant social relationship can be automatically transformed into a productive and satisfying relationship between client and consultant.

Table 3.1. The client's concerns

What it feels like to be a buyer

1. I'm feeling **insecure**. I'm not sure I know how to detect which of the finalists is the genius and which is just good. I've exhausted my abilities to make technical distinctions.

2. I'm feeling **threatened**. This is my area of responsibility, and even though intellectually I know I need outside expertise, emotionally it's not comfortable to put my affairs in the hands of others.

3. I'm taking a **personal risk**. By putting my affairs in the hands of someone else, I risk losing control.

4. I'm **impatient**. I didn't call in someone at the first sign of symptoms (or opportunity). I've been thinking about this for a while.

5. I'm **worried**. By the very fact of suggesting improvements or changes, these people are going to be implying that I haven't been doing it right up till now. Are these people going to be on my side?

6. I'm **exposed**. Whoever I hire, I'm going to reveal some proprietary secrets, not all of which are flattering. I will have to undress.

7. I'm feeling **ignorant**, and don't like the feeling. I don't know if I've got a simple problem or a complex one. I'm not sure I can trust them to be honest about that: it's in their interest to convince me it's complex.

8. I'm **sceptical**. I've been burned before by these kinds of people. You get a lot of promises: How do I know whose promise I should buy?

9. I'm **concerned** that they either can't or won't take the time to understand what makes my situation special. They'll try to sell me what they've got rather than what I need.

10. I'm **suspicious**. Will they be those typical professionals who are hard to get hold of, who are patronizing, who leave you out of the loop, who befuddle you with jargon, who don't explain what they are doing or why, who..., who..., who...? In short, will these people deal with me in the way I want to be dealt with?

Source: David Maister: *How clients choose* (Boston, Massachusetts, David H. Maister Associates, 1991).

Assignment design

Observers of consulting tend to agree that it would not be enough to find a consultant who is competent in general terms. The firm's and the individual consultant's competence must be demonstrated by their approach to the assignment for which the selection is being made. This approach will reveal if the consultant:

○   has taken the trouble to fully understand the client's real and unique problem;

○   is suggesting a new and creative way of handling the client's problem, or is merely proposing to use one of his firm's standard packages;

o   is submitting a proposal that is superior to what other consultants have
    envisaged;

o   is suggesting something that will really make a difference;

o   has designed the assignment as a modern-type consultancy, to maximize
    the client's participation and learning at all stages of the job;

o   has chosen the most efficient and cheapest way of planning, structuring
    and staffing the assignment without reducing quality.

There are two main sources of information for evaluating assignment
design: discussions with the consultant concerning your problem and the ways
in which it can be approached and solutions sought, and a formal assignment
proposal submitted by the consultant.

Both sources should be used and complement each other. If a formal
selection procedure is used (see Chapter 4), the consultant submits a proposal
based on terms of reference and other criteria set in a letter of invitation. In
addition, there should be some discussions with the consultant at various
stages of assignment preparation and negotiation. Interviews concerning the
winning proposals should be quite detailed.

If there is no formal procedure, the client may be satisfied by having
reviewed the consultant's approach informally in one or more meetings.
However, it is advisable to ask for a brief written proposal in any case, to confirm the results of informal discussions, avoid the risk of misunderstanding,
and inform others in both organizations on what has been agreed.

Capability to deliver

The consultant must be able to deliver what he has promised. An obvious requirement is that competent consultant staff must be available at the
right time. Logistic, backstopping and supervisory capabilities are also important, in particular in complex international assignments. For example, will the
firm be able to operate effectively in a foreign country where it has no office,
no liaison agent, no local collaborating firm and no administrative support
service? It may be that a local firm would stand a better chance, or the foreign consultant should be encouraged to join forces with a local consultant,
who can provide local support and take care of tasks for which it is not necessary to fly in an expensive foreign expert.

Some consultants bid for assignments that they are not able to deliver
with their own resources. The client can find out about this quite easily by
examining the proposal received, asking a few direct questions and inquiring
about the consulting firm. For example, a small generalist consulting firm will
propose to use two specialist firms as subcontractors or to share the assign-

ment with a consultant in another country, with whom it has a cooperation agreement. These and similar formulas are practised quite frequently and may be fully acceptable if discussed openly and agreed with the client.

Ability to mobilize further resources

In complex and open-ended assignments, the need to go beyond the agreed scope of the assignment may be identified in the course of operations. As a client, you will want to know if you will have to look yourself for further resources, such as special engineering advice, market information, legal advice or intermediaries for finding business partners. Most consultants will tell you (and this information may be correct) that they can find any further expertise and resources that may be needed for the project. There will, however, be two questions: (a) can they find the best available resources for a reasonable price; and (b) if they are in a leadership position as your principal project advisers and suppliers of expertise, will they be accepted by other advisers and intermediaries as leaders and coordinators?

The cost of consulting services

Both management consultants and experienced clients tend to agree that cost considerations should not dominate selection and prevail over competence, quality and excellent rapport with the consultant. This view is shared by consultants in various professions: for example, the International Federation of Consulting Engineers (FIDIC) recommends clients to select consulting engineers "by ability and not by price competition", using the criteria of technical competence, managerial ability, availability of resources, professional independence, fairness of fee structure and professional integrity.[1] Yet cost is not unimportant to clients, and few of them can afford to ignore it in selection.

To take the fee level and structure into consideration is fully justified. You want to be sure that the consultant applies fee rates and charges fees in accordance with the profession's normal practice and that the ways of charging fees are agreed upon before the start of the assignment. If the consultant's fees are higher, you want to know the reason and consider if you can agree to it.

You want to know the reasons for lower than average fee levels as well:

o   Is it the consultant's general pricing policy or is he making an exception in order to get your assignment? Why does he need to make an exception? Is his firm in difficulties or is it a marketing gimmick?

o   Is the consultant employing less competent staff and paying them lower salaries?

o   Does the consultant come from a lower-cost and lower-income country, where lower fees are practised in professional services?

o   Do the lower fees reflect the size and structure of the consulting firm, which is able to operate efficiently with lower overhead expenses?

The fee formula, i.e. the technique of calculating and charging fees (see Chapter 5), may also be a factor of selection in some cases. For example, a client may prefer to pay a per-unit-of-time (time-based) fee, while a consultant likes to charge a flat fee.

An analysis of the fee requested often reveals issues of assignment design and staffing that ought to be discussed with the consultant:

o   the consultant may have suggested an approach that is too costly (e.g. extensive data collection, using larger samples than necessary, elaboration of too many alternatives, purchasing expensive proprietary systems or hardware, etc.);

o   the assignment proposal may foresee the use of higher and more costly expertise (more senior consultants) than actually needed for the task;

o   consultants often suggest the use of their own staff for jobs that the client could easily do with (or even without) some training and guidance.

If a flat-rate (lump sum) fee is proposed for the whole job, it may be useful to review with the consultant the criteria used to determine the price. In consulting, there are always some time considerations behind a flat-rate fee. For example, if the fee is US$100,000, the consultant's thinking may have been as follows: "most probably I will need 40 days at US$1,500 each. Then there will be a charge of US$15,000 for proprietary know-how and some other expenses. This leaves US$25,000. If I do the job in 40 days, this will be a good extra profit. But what is the probability that I will have to spend more than 40 days without being able to charge them to the client? If the probability is high, I am taking a big risk and the fee is justified. If it is pretty sure that I will not take more than 40 days, I am probably overcharging and the client may challenge my price – if he is able to do so".

The reputation or image of the consultant

To turn to a reputable professional firm is the easiest thing to do. It is the obvious choice for many inexperienced users of consultants, who want to avoid a difficult and risky selection. Some decision-makers in the public sector prefer to turn to firms of high repute in order to avoid any possible criticism and accusation of corruption.

Reputation or image is how the client circles and even the general public view the consultant. Some clients may know nothing more than the name and believe that behind it there is unquestionable professional expertise and integrity. To others the image is more specific and colourful, since they have heard about the firm's achievements and possibly also misfortunes. It is good to know that hardly any professional firm has a simple and absolutely pure image, and that image occasionally gets distorted and biased by publicity campaigns, eulogistic or destructive press articles, and spectacular cases of success or failure.

The consultant's reputation or image is a surrogate to be used if you cannot use other more specific and reliable criteria, or in order to complete and supplement these criteria.

Weighing and combining the criteria

The criteria reviewed in the previous paragraphs are summarized in table 3.2 for the reader's convenience. In business practice there are many different clients and assignments. Therefore it is not possible to develop a simple blueprint for applying these criteria. Three factors will play a key role:

o   the availability of information related to particular criteria. If you lack information on how consultants charge for their services or what should be included in a properly presented assignment proposal, how do you want to assess the candidates for your assignment?

o   the client's ability to draw conclusions from available information. It is not evident that, given enough information on two consultants, a client will be able to identify the more suitable one. Consultant selection is a skill that can be based to some extent on a rigorous approach, but that also involves a great deal of experience in telling the difference between professionalism and mediocrity;

o   the client's attitude to various criteria whereby consultants can be judged. Thus, a good rapport with the consultant developed in previous assignments may outweigh all other criteria.

If a client aims to be as rigorous and consistent as possible and to use all the criteria reviewed above, a question of priorities and weights will arise. Depending on circumstances, you may decide that:

o   some criteria will be treated as conditions (only consultants who meet them will be eligible);

o   other criteria will be used for determining the order of priority in which consultants are eligible;

Table 3.2. Consultant selection criteria – Checklist

1. **Professional integrity**
   (code of ethics and conduct)

2. **Professional competence**
   - Firm's and individual consultant's competence
   - Knowledge of industry
   - Understanding of country and culture
   - Hard and soft skills
   - Creativity and innovation

3. **Rapport with the consultant**
   (from former work, newly established, social contacts)

4. **Assignment design**
   (quality, imagination, participative approach, efficiency)

5. **Capability to deliver**
   (availability of resources, right timing)

6. **Ability to mobilize resources**
   (contacts within and outside professions, credibility, negotiation skills)

7. **Cost of services**
   (fee level and formula)

8. **Image of consultant**
   (reputation in business and professional circles)

○   the remaining criteria may be either disregarded or used to complete the picture, or may help to decide if criteria of the second group do not suffice.

In formal consultant selection procedures, it is customary to select a smaller number of criteria (three to five) and assign weights to them, in order to tell the consultants in advance how they will be judged and make sure that a collectively made selection will achieve some degree of homogeneity and consistency. Some examples will be given in the following chapter.

An emerging criterion: Quality certification

Since 1990-91, consulting firms in several countries have been encouraged to seek formal certification, confirming that their policies, resources and practices comply with international quality standards such as ISO 9001, or corresponding national norms, such as BS 5750 in the United Kingdom. At the time of writing, only a negligible number of consultancies have completed the mandatory review and certification procedure and obtained quality certificates from authorized bodies. However, quite a few consultants are actively pursuing quality certification with the support of their associations. It can be expected that, in future years, certificates of quality will increasingly be required by clients in drawing up consultants' shortlists and choosing consultants for particular assignments.

3.3. The impact of marketing of consulting services

When a client starts thinking of choosing a consultant, his mind is never a blank sheet even if he has no direct personal experience with the use of consultants. The reason is simple: management and other consultants are very active at marketing and, at the present time, expend more and more efforts and resources on it. When you decide to recruit a consultant, you have already been exposed to a lot of marketing by some, but not all, of your prospects. Marketing brings to you the knowledge of the leading actors on the consulting scene and provides you with some insights into what is going on in management and consulting. You may not realize it, but your mind may have been strongly conditioned by marketing: you view a consulting firm through a book published under its name, a large-format advertisement in your preferred business journal, an interesting survey compiled by the consultant for firms in your industry or a courtesy visit that a senior partner has paid you.

Indirect marketing

Indirect marketing does not address any specific client but a wide business community including existing and potential clients. Consultants use many tools, including advertisements, meetings and conferences, public speeches, books, articles, information pamphlets and guides, newsletters, mailing campaigns, donations for social purposes, sponsorship of research projects and so on. The objective is to create and enhance a consulting firm's professional reputation and image. Indirect marketing markets the firm, not a particular assignment. The purpose is to influence the clients' minds and impress on them that they do not have to worry if they have a problem, because there is a consulting firm that will help them out of trouble. Through indirect marketing, consultants are trying to convince you that:

o   their work is at the cutting edge of science and technology;

o   they possess or can mobilize vast resources in all possible areas of know-how that you may need;

o   they have developed some extremely effective diagnostic, information processing, project management, planning and other methodologies;

o   they treat each client with the same attention and care;

o   they do not sell uniform products but devise unique solutions for every single client;

o   their approach is different from other consultants, and so on.

Different marketing techniques will appeal to different clients. You should be aware of your own preferences and values. If you like to scan pamphlets on recent developments in business and technology and you are regularly receiving them from one consulting firm, you may have developed a preference for this firm. Through indirect marketing, you can gain helpful information on the consulting profession and business. You can form your own opinion on the quality of output (such as information pamphlets and guides) of various consulting firms. You will also receive a lot of useless publicity that does not deserve your attention and should be screened by your assistant who is in charge of daily mail.

Direct marketing

The consultant's marketing is called direct if he approaches your firm to establish a rapport, offer a service and sell an assignment. A great deal of information and publicity material is mailed direct to you by various consulting firms and training institutions. If it is standard printed material, it is at the limit between indirect and direct marketing, since the same material is normally distributed to hundreds or thousands of addresses. However, such mailing is often followed by a more personal letter, a telephone call or a request for an appointment by the firm's senior representative, or your friend or business acquaintance is asked by a consultant to introduce him to you. Is it useful to agree to such contacts, will they help you in choosing consultants and is it worth spending time on them?

Receiving visits made for the sole purpose of introducing the consulting firm is not particularly interesting unless the consultant is an exceptional person and you know in advance that you will learn something new. Therefore, if a consultant wants to see you, he should be encouraged to prepare himself for the meeting and think of information that you may need, or of a new product used elsewhere that might also be of interest to your firm. You may then decide on the level, focus and composition of the meeting. Many consultants want to see the top executive although their message actually concerns and can be handled by a quite different person in the organization.

If a consultant is already working for your firm, it is reasonable to assume that he is thinking of marketing a new assignment to you while working on a current one. This is common practice in consulting. An inside knowledge of your organization and contacts with your people will help him in this. However, you will want to stay in charge and control the relationship. As mentioned, an excellent rapport with the consultant may be a valid reason for choosing him again for another task. Yet you do not want to be exposed to any pressure. No consultant has the right to think that the next contract is "in the bag" because he is already working with your organization.

3.4. General sources of information on consulting and consultants

Although you have been exposed to some consultant's marketing and this has probably influenced your opinion, you may wish to take a wider look at what is available, collecting and evaluating information that has been defined by you, not by one or more prospective consultants. This section will point out some general sources of information on consulting and consultants.

Information on the consulting profession and practices

Before talking to any consulting firm about a specific assignment, it is good to have a fairly up-to-date and balanced picture of the consulting profession. It is useful to know that there are different consulting approaches, styles, organizations, contracting and fee-setting practices, and so on. A publication such as this provides a useful overview. It is, however, focused on selection and use by clients. In addition, you may be interested in reading more about the consulting profession and even some related professions, such as auditing and accounting. Professional associations will be pleased to provide you with information. Most of them have produced pamphlets on how to approach their members and use their services. The German association BDU has produced guidelines for clients on how to tell the difference between "serious and not serious behaviour" of a management consultant. Readers who are interested in seeing other sources of information on the profession and its trends may find some suggestions in Appendix 2. In addition, you can attend a consultants' conference or workshop, which is a good opportunity to hear about consultants' achievements and problems and share experiences with them.

Directories

Every consultants' association and institute (see Appendix 1) will provide a list or directory of members, showing their areas of consulting expertise and/or examples of typical assignments, and in some cases also short statements of the firm's consulting philosophy. Firms that are not members will not be listed.

There are, furthermore, a few commercial publishers of directories of consultants and other professional services (see Appendix 2). As a rule, a consultant will be listed if he finds the directory useful and agrees to pay a fee to the publisher. There is no screening – whoever applies and provides the requested information gets listed.

Telephone directories (the Yellow Pages or trade section) are another source where some addresses and a limited amount of information on consultants and other professionals can be found.

Absolutely complete and reliable directories do not exist. Directories are of some use, for example, if you are looking for a consultant in a very special field, or for one who has offices in a particular locality. They are tools of basic information, not of selection.

Information provided by associations

In addition to publishing and distributing directories of members, the associations of consultants are able to give some information on member firms to potential clients. A client can visit or call the association's secretariat and describe the assignment for which he wants to find a consultant. The association would provide, informally and on a confidential basis, names of three to six member firms that may be suitable. Some associations, such as the Institute of Management Consultants in the United Kingdom, operate a client inquiry service, helping to identify consultants among firms meeting certain criteria. However, there also are associations that do not wish to give such information and confine themselves to providing a members' directory. This is understandable owing to the small staff at the associations' secretariats and to possible objections by members who might feel discriminated against if they find that names of other firms have been suggested more frequently than their own.

Agencies for locating consultants

Independent agencies and services that can help clients to locate and evaluate consultants are rare. Some examples are described in Appendix 2. In countries where the consulting market is new, and clients have both little experience with the use of consultants and limited information on what is available there is scope for creating such services in employers' organizations or chambers of commerce, or as private organizations. To be useful to potential clients, they must be technically competent and totally independent and objective.

Rosters

Rosters of consultants are lists or data banks compiled in order to facilitate search to a certain group of users. For example, the World Bank and other development banks have rosters from which staff members and borrowers can choose. In the public sector of various countries, ministries that are frequent users of consultants may have their own rosters, or there may be a common roster in the government purchasing unit, ministry of finance or other central department.

A roster of consultants can be of some help if it is not a simple list of names and addresses compiled in a haphazard way, for example by including every firm that requests registration or copying names from directories. Some practical criterion has to be chosen in structuring and compiling the roster, which should include information on who used the consultant and can provide references, and on strong and weak points of various firms.

Unfortunately, most rosters are little more than incomplete lists of names. Organizations keeping rosters are well aware of this and warn potential clients against misuse. Also, rosters should not be used to restrict selection by preventing a client from considering consultants who are not on the roster.

3.5. Gathering and using information on individual consultants

Detailed information on selected firms may be required for various reasons. You may think of developing your own private roster or data bank on consultants, or you are already looking for precise information on one or a few firms to be considered for an assignment. The following sources and methods may be of help.

Information from other clients and business contacts

Word of mouth is the oldest, simplest, yet most useful and reliable way of getting information on professional service firms. Consultants are well aware of this and attach a great deal of importance to the impressions that clients share with each other. To a consultant, a happy client is the most effective and least expensive marketing tool.

In searching for a management consultant or another professional firm, it is useful to start by talking to people whom you know and whose judgement you respect. They may be your personal friends and colleagues, business contacts, bankers, lawyers, auditors and others who have some experience with professional services. Obviously, you will be cautious in using suggestions from people whom you hardly know or whose judgement leaves you uncertain.

Furthermore, consultants normally provide referrals. These are names of firms and managers for whom the consultant has done some work and who have given permission to mention this work to future clients. Most clients just scan the list of referrals provided by the consultant and are happy to see names of known companies. However, the purpose of referrals is to facilitate direct communication between clients. Therefore do not hesitate to speak to the consultant's former clients, asking specific questions. They will be pleased to share experience with you and you may be surprised how much useful advice you can gain.

Written documentation and publications provided by consulting firms

Every consulting firm can provide a brochure or flyer describing its services. It is often an elegant and costly product, designed and distributed for marketing purposes. Informed clients are not impressed by the layout and the quality of paper. They seek usable technical information, but in most cases find little of it. Yet these brochures are not completely useless if the consultants are able to anticipate questions normally asked by potential clients.

Another source is a capability statement or technical memorandum. These documents describing the firm's profile, background and capabilities are normally enclosed with assignment proposals, or provided to clients who are looking for more information on consultants in order to make a pre-selection and draw up a short-list (see also section 4.1). This group of documents is more focused and specific than the previous one since it is produced with a particular client's requirements in mind. However, although this may be an advantage, it may also give an incomplete picture. Furthermore, some consultants do not really bother producing focused capability statements and provide standard material instead.

Technical publications (books, papers, special reports, pamphlets, articles) reflecting on the consultant's research and experience are much more interesting. Their purpose is to demonstrate to current and potential clients that the consultant can make a unique contribution and that he is already making some of his know-how publicly available. It is of course necessary to look at the real value of the publication. Any consultant can produce a basic guide to doing business in central and eastern Europe and the market is already flooded by such guides. A practical guide on how to harmonize management cultures and styles of western and eastern companies that have decided to merge or cooperate would be another matter, but so far no consultant has published such a guide.

Interviewing the consultant

Interviewing is one of the principal techniques used in consulting; therefore most consultants are masters of interviewing. Nevertheless, as a potential client you should not hesitate to interview your consultant. This requires skill and preparation, because it is right to assume that your interviewee is an experienced interviewer.[2]

The interview can be structured (directive) or unstructured (non-directive), or both. Several people in your organization can interview the consultant separately. Structured interviews will follow a list of specific questions concerning the consulting firm and the consultant whom you are interviewing, their expertise, past and current clients, methods of intervention, the general business climate and trends, the situation in the profession and the sector to which your organization belongs, the approach to your assignment, and so on. Information already submitted by the consultant would be examined before the interview in order to avoid repetition and focus the interview on obtaining further and more specific information, including the consultant's views and feelings on important economic and business issues and on problems faced by your company.

An unstructured interview can also be useful if it occurs spontaneously when you meet the consultant at a professional gathering or socially. In this case, it is preferable to use broad and open questions, giving the consultant the opportunity to demonstrate his perspective and breadth of understanding of complex concepts and situations. Unstructured interviewing can be time-consuming and unproductive, since it may wander over a wide range of general topics and it may be difficult to ask specific and detailed questions.

Table 3.3 suggests some questions that might be used in interviewing consultants. You may, of course, be able to think of many other questions. Since your interviewee is a management consultant, you will probably not meet any resistance even if you ask a clumsy or awkward question. However, you may be getting evasive answers and will have to find out if this is due to your way of asking questions, or the consultant's inability or reluctance to give proper answers. Some useful principles of effective interviewing are summarized in table 3.4.

Observing the consultant in action

It would be ideal if you could see the consultant at work, doing the same things that you want him to do in your organization. This is seldom possible. Yet you can observe the consultant, and learn a great deal about his technical expertise, personality and behaviour:

o when he is a speaker or discussion leader in public conferences and workshops;

Table 3.3. Some questions for interviewing consultants

- Why are you interested in our company?
- What do you think about our problems and prospects?
- What are your experience and resources for work in our sector?
- How would you tackle our problem?
- What previous experience can you use in our assignment?
- What has been your professional career?
- What makes your services different from those of other consultants?
- What services other than consulting can you provide or help to identify?
- How do you collaborate with other professional firms?
- What methods of consulting do you prefer to use?
- How do you structure, staff and control consulting projects?
- When was your firm established and how did it grow?
- In what countries and technical areas does your firm operate?
- What is your firm's and your personal consulting philosophy?
- What is your firm's business strategy?
- Who are your principal clients? How do you choose them?
- What marketing techniques do you use?
- What referrals would you like to provide?
- Can you describe your most and least successful assignments?
- What are the main strengths and weaknesses of your firm?
- How is your firm managed? Who owns and controls your firm?
- What problems worry your firm's management most?
- What do you think about the state of the consulting profession? What should change in the profession?
- Are you a member of a consulting association?
- What fee formulas do you regard as appropriate?
- Do you see any risk of conflicts of interests if you work with us on this assignment?

Note: Depending on the context, any question can be worded differently, made more specific and pursued in more detail.

Table 3.4. Basic principles of interviewing

- Start the interview in a pleasant and relaxed atmosphere, if possible in a room where you will be free from interruptions.

- Make sure that you break the ice at the opening of the interview.

- Prepare your questions, but be ready to modify the list and change the sequence of questions during the interview.

- Be alert to non-verbal messages, feelings and impressions.

- Note facts during the interview (with the interviewee's agreement), note impressions and feelings after the interview.

- Encourage a spontaneous flow of information by asking further questions and showing interest by smiling, nodding, mentioning that information is really interesting and new to you, etc.

- Do not dominate the conversation, avoid interrupting, arguing, stating your own opinions and criticizing the statements of the interviewee.

- When the questions are answered vaguely, pursue them in a non-aggressive and pleasant way until they are fully clarified.

- Refrain from asking strong and direct questions too early in the interview; however, do not hesitate to ask them when you feel that the time is appropriate.

---

o during presentations and meetings in your organization;

o in contract negotiations;

o in informal personal contacts;

o while interviewing the consultant;

o during smaller assignments.

By observing the consultant in action you will learn about his flexibility and self-control. Does he easily adjust to unforeseen situations? Does he try to impose his prepared agenda on you and sell packaged programmes or does he flexibly react to your questions and priorities? Can he adjust his approach? Can he control his temper if someone irritates him? Does he listen carefully? Is he patient and tolerant, but persevering and consistent?

Testing the consultant at small tasks

Before selecting a new consultant for an important assignment, it may be possible to test him through smaller jobs: a diagnostic study in one unit or plant, an opinion survey, a half-day workshop with your staff on a topic of interest, an independent assessment of project proposals prepared by other

---

consultants or your staff, a survey of state-of-the art techniques applicable to your case, and the like. Keep in mind the main purpose of the test: is it checking technical expertise or the consultant's interpersonal skills? Also, the consultant should not feel that he is being given a meaningless job just to be checked. The task should be real and useful to your organization and should be treated as a regular short-term assignment.

In certain instances, it may be possible to select the consultant for the first phase of the assignment, and confirm the selection for the next phases only when it becomes clear that the consultant's performance has been satisfactory. The design of the assignment must permit a change of consultant in the middle of the job, say after the diagnostic phase. Otherwise it will be obvious that the consultant's selection will be confirmed in any case if performance is better than disastrous.

Your company's records

In the previous paragraphs, we have reviewed a number of sources and techniques for collecting and evaluating detailed information on individual consultants. Clearly, you do not want to repeat the same cumbersome search each time your company needs a consultant. You want to have information at hand and be able to use it quickly. There is no other way than to establish and maintain reliable internal records, which would be available to every decision-maker, or "problem owner", who may be contemplating the use of a consultant.

The following documentation may be kept in the records:

o   a few pieces of basic information on consultants (books, special reports, newspaper cuttings, documentation received from consultants' associations);

o   documentation related to consulting contracts (samples of terms of reference, letters of invitation, contract texts, guidelines for drafting contracts);

o   selected documentation on firms regarded as particularly interesting, including suggestions received from friends and business colleagues, and reports on interviews of consultants;

o   short internal reports on assignments completed in your company (produced by you, not the consultant, but also summarizing your consultants' views on how you have worked with them, as will be discussed in section 8.3);

o   short notes on consultants who have applied for assignments but have not been selected (it is useful to note why applicants could not be selected in a previous case in order to separate consultants who were evaluated and regarded as unsuitable from those who could not be retained for one assignment, but belong to the pool of interesting candidates for future assignments).

Your internal documentation may well become the main and most reliable source of intelligence for choosing your consultants.

---

[1] FIDIC: *Selection by ability: FIDIC guidelines on the selection of consulting engineers* (Lausanne).

[2] See J. Quay: *Diagnostic interviewing for consultants and auditors* (Columbus, Ohio, Quay Associates, 1986); or M. Kubr and J. Prokopenko: *Diagnosing management training and development needs: Concepts and techniques* (Geneva, ILO, 1989), pp. 101-108.

ON CONSULTANT SELECTION PROCEDURES

4

This chapter will describe a formal procedure used to select consultants. To some clients this procedure may look excessively detailed and cumbersome. If you are an owner of a smaller enterprise, no one can force you to follow any complex procedure for choosing a consultant. Even many large organizations in the private sector have no formal procedure for consultant selection. Case by case, management decides in what way and on what terms it would appoint a consultant. Informal ways of selecting consultants and other professional advisers prevail.

Our objective is not to convince you that, after having read this book, you should adopt a more structured and elaborate procedure for choosing consultants for your organization. If you have been satisfied by an informal approach, stick to it. Yet it is useful to know the steps and activities involved in a complete consultant selection procedure, because this knowledge, and the application of some of its elements, can greatly increase the quality of informal selection. For example, even if the process is essentially informal it is useful to have a well-structured written proposal from the consultant describing the job he proposes to do for you.

In public agencies, both national and international, the use of standardized formal selection procedures prevails. The procedure may be mandatory or recommended. There may be an official document, issued by a government agency, which describes the procedure and method of consultant selection and provides a lot of additional information and guidelines, including forms and outlines of consultant contracts and the like.

The reasons for the use of formal procedures in the puiblic sector can be summarized as follows:

o   to give all eligible candidates the same chance;

o   to increase the probability of identification and choice of the most suitable consultant;

o   to make selection "transparent" and less prone to criticism, and to reduce the risks of favouritism, nepotism and corruption;

○ to harmonize the approaches used and transfer good experience among various government departments and public agencies;

○ to generally improve the quality of consultant selection and appointment in a complex public sector environment.

As with any other procedure, a consultant selection procedure can be used poorly or even misused. To solicit proposals from several consultants is of no help if the choice will be in the hands of a panel composed of incompetent people; or a decision-maker can refer to the use of a procedure to justify the fairness of selection although in reality the choice was pre-arranged and biased. A well-defined procedure helps, but there is no substitute for the competence and honesty of those who are using it. However, participating in a procedure (e.g. by drafting terms of reference, preselecting candidates or examining proposals) educates clients and their staff in the practices of consulting and in problem identification and diagnosis. This can be a significant benefit.

4.1. A typical procedure

Many different procedures can be seen at work in various countries and agencies. They reflect local experience and traditions, and the requirements of legislation. Yet they exhibit significant similarities and, therefore, we have chosen to outline a typical procedure, which can serve as a model for assessing and improving consultant selection procedures used in particular countries and agencies. Our model includes nine steps as shown in table 4.1. Each step will be briefly reviewed and supplemented by a checklist if appropriate.

Table 4.1. **Principal steps of consultant selection procedure**

(1) Terms of reference

(2) Resource and procedure authorization

(3) Short-listing (preselection)

(4) Invitation to submit proposals

(5) Preparation and submission of proposals

(6) Evaluation of proposals

(7) Contract negotiation

(8) Selection

(9) Contract finalization and signature

Step 1 – Terms of reference

The selection procedure starts by drafting the terms of reference for the assignment. As discussed in detail in section 2.3, the terms of reference provide the client's definition of the problem and the sort of help that will be sought from consultants. They show how far the client was able to go in identifying and describing his problem and the need for a consultancy. Therefore they signal to the consultants what nature of intervention will be required. If the situation of the client organization is uncertain and the client was not in a position to produce clear and precise terms of reference, the consultant will understand from these terms that a lot more diagnostic and conceptual work will be needed and that the job eventually to be done may be quite different from that outlined in the terms of reference.

Some clients may choose to use consultants for drafting the terms of reference. Usually this is done in important engineering projects and in situations where a lot of fact finding, analytical and drafting work needs to be carried out in order to define the scope of the assignment. In such cases, the procedure may stipulate that the author of the terms of reference cannot bid for project execution. This restriction may be waived in certain cases, in particular if in drafting the terms of reference the consultant has demonstrated that he is obviously very suitable for the job and not admitting his name to the short-list would actually deprive the client firm of an excellent candidate.

Step 2 – Resource and procedure authorization

Once the need for a consultancy has been identified and the terms of reference drafted, it has to be decided under what circumstances and in what way the consultancy will be prepared, negotiated, agreed and implemented. Formal decisions or informal agreements may have to be obtained internally within the client organization (from higher management or from the board of directors) and/or externally (from a ministry, a bank providing a loan or a technical assistance agency).

The need for approval and authorization may concern the draft terms of reference, the definitive or indicative amount of money needed for financing the assignment, the conditions of financing, the details of the procedure to be used, and the definition of authority and responsibility, including the appointment of individuals and committees which will manage and implement the procedure. Furthermore, the authorizing body may reserve certain roles for itself in order to keep control of the fairness of the procedure and of resource commitments. In section 4.2 we shall see that this is normal practice of several development banks.

At this point the client organization would designate the chairman and members of a consultant appointment or selection board (panel, committee).

The board should include members who are sufficiently knowledgeable about the problem area covered by the assignment, as well as about organizational and consultant selection procedures. It may be necessary to arrange special briefing or training sessions for new and inexperienced board members. Managers or specialists who would regard their functions on the board as unimportant and would not be able to study the consultants' proposals, participate in interviews, and so on, should not be used as members of selection boards.

When appointed, the board takes charge of the selection procedure, but the board chairman keeps in mind the need to consult managers and specialists who are not members of the board, and to seek approval of decisions that are not within the board's authority.

Step 3 – Short-listing

Short-listing is consultant preselection. The purpose is to identify suitable candidates who might be interested and capable of doing the job. Another purpose is rationality – it would not make much sense and would be extremely costly and cumbersome to ask hundreds of candidates to prepare and submit proposals. While the task could become unmanageable to you, it would also cause a lot of unnecessary work and expenditure to many consultants. As a rule, your short-list will include three to six names (with some names on a reserve list).

From previous projects and contacts with consultants you may already have an obvious short-list. This will also be the case if the job is very specialized and only a small number of consulting firms that are known to you come into consideration. For many jobs of a more general nature the theoretical pool of potential candidates will include hundreds of candidates and you will have to reduce this number, using the criteria and techniques discussed in Chapter 3. You will have to decide what criteria to apply and from what basic pool you will be seeking your candidates.

Short-listing can be done as a fairly open exercise, involving contacts with the consultants. They can be asked informally to provide information that would justify their inclusion in the short-list. You may be able to interview some of them and should not miss the chance to do so. The consultants who talk to you at this stage should not be induced to believe that they have already received a higher rating than their competitors, or that they can exert any influence on the selection procedure. The contacts are clearly preliminary and informative.

If a public project of some importance is being prepared, it may be mandatory to publish a public announcement in the press, requesting interested consultants to contact the client and provide information justifying their short-listing. They will have to send you a technical memorandum, or capability statement, which should include enough specific information on the profile of the consultant to be of real use in short-listing.

Step 4 – Invitation to submit proposals

The short-listed candidates will be invited in writing to submit proposals (tenders). They will receive a complete set of information and documentation needed to prepare the proposal and submit it in a form and time fixed by the client. Table 4.2 gives a checklist of information required in a letter of invitation.

Table 4.2. Letter of invitation – Checklist

- Invitation to participate in tendering and submit a proposal
- Information on selection procedure and criteria used in appraising proposals
- Terms of reference
- Estimate of the work volume and/or financial limit (if appropriate)
- Additional information on client organization, project setting and source of financing
- Invitation to attend briefings (if any)
- Indication of further information to be obtained on request
- Invitation to contact the client for further information and fact-finding
- Clear and detailed description of the required content, structuring and presentation of the proposal (including maximum length if appropriate)
- Required presentation, justification and currency of price and other financial information
- Anticipated starting date
- Period for which the consultant's offer (price, staffing, organization) is to be held valid
- Information on interviewing and contract negotiations with preselected candidates
- Names and addresses of the firms invited (optional)
- Submission deadline, addresses, number of copies, form of presentation and transmission, budgets presented separately or not, envelopes sealed or not
- Request to confirm reception of this letter and inform whether the consultant will tender
- Any other conditions and criteria to be met by the proposal
- Courtesy formulas

Note: Information listed here can be in the body of the letter or in annexes.

The scope and style of a letter of invitation will reflect the client's habits and preference. Information can be provided in the main text of the letter or in annexes. For example, the TOR could be part of the letter, but in most cases would be provided in an annex.

If voluminous documentation is available in the client organization to interested consultants and it is not practical to send it to every prospect, the letter would invite consultants to visit the client organization. This invitation might be made in the letter anyway, in particular if further fact-finding, personal contacts and discussions are clearly required for preparing good-quality proposals. In preparing for important consultancies, some clients invite short-listed consultants to briefing sessions at which the project is presented in detail, questions are answered and further appointments arranged for fact-finding and diagnosis.

It is important that at this stage you think of all information that you want to get from the consultant to be able to judge his proposal and the suitability of the firm for your job. This is particularly important in international consulting, since the supply of professional services is not governed by standard international rules and what may be normal practice in your country may come as a surprise to a foreign consultant. It is too late to make unpleasant discoveries due to lack of information when one candidate has been selected and you are about to sign the contract.

Step 5 – Preparation and submission of proposals

During this phase the workload shifts to the consultants who have accepted the invitation to submit proposals. In a relatively short time (one to three months in most cases) they will have to study the terms of reference, the supporting documentation and the conditions of the assignment, and then prepare and submit their proposals. At least some of the candidates, if not all, may decide to visit the client organization to make their own preliminary diagnosis and check if they have all the information needed for developing a proposal which stands a good chance. To the client, these visits provide another opportunity to meet the prospective consultants and see how they collect facts, identify problems and deal with people in an organizational environment that is new to them.

In preparing for an important assignment, a consultant may need to spend several days in intensive discussions and studying documents and data at the client organization. This is in line with the basic principles of the consulting approach. In order to be able to draft a realistic proposal tailored to your situation and not merely copied from some previous assignments, the consultant must be sure that he can subscribe to your definition of the problem as given to him in the TOR, and can supplement your preliminary fact-finding by his own investigation and talking to people to understand your culture, motivation, constraints, competence of key people, and so on.

There are practical implications, however. Inviting ten consulting firms to tender may imply that you would receive ten visits from different firms within two to three weeks. They will have to send fairly senior people, versed in quick assessments of client organizations and able to think of assignment design and strategy after a few interviews with the client's staff. On the client's side, competent people have to be available for these contacts. The question is what you can afford and are able to cope with. Also, if too many candidates are invited and know about it, they may regard their chance as slim and decide not to spend much effort on your proposal. With ten candidates you may have more work but poorer results than with three or five.

It is essential that the consultant and the client compare their perceptions, definitions used and expectations. Terms such as "master plan", "system diagnosis", "restructuring", "organization development" and others lend themselves to many interpretations, and the consultant should be able to find out what exactly the client has in mind. It is useful to ask the consultant if he fully understands the letter of invitation, including the concepts and terms used, and if he feels that anything has been left out. Consultants have more experience with selection procedures than most clients. Many consultants have their own checklists, which can be compared with your checklist.

The depth and degree of detail of the consultant's assignment proposal can also be a source of misunderstanding. The consultant may worry, and rightly, that by submitting a very detailed proposal he is already providing the solution or a part of it. As a result, the client might thank the consultant for the proposal, and if in this way he has collected four or five solid and detailed proposals, he may be able to cancel the assignment or restructure it totally, since he has gathered enough free advice by talking to the consultants and receiving very detailed proposals from them.

As regards the layout and form of presentation of proposals, the needs and wishes of the client have priority before the practices and convenience of the consultant. The consultants must take account of the fact that, to the client and his staff, this may be the first important case of consultant selection and that the proposals must lend themselves to easy reading, comparison and assessment using the client's know-how and criteria. Consultants who respect these criteria scrupulously, also using the client's technical language and not their own jargon, stand a better chance. This will not prevent them from including new ideas in the proposal to demonstrate that their approach is superior to that of their competitors, and attractive to the client.

Step 5 is completed when the client receives the proposals as stipulated in the letter of invitation (number of copies, whether budgets should be submitted separately from the technical proposals, whether sealed envelopes should be used, etc.).

Information to be included in a consultant's proposal to a client can be grouped under four headings described in more detail in table 4.3:

(1) Approach to the assignment.

(2) Staffing and backstopping.

(3) Profile and background of firm.

(4) Fees and other terms.

Table 4.3. Assignment proposal – Checklist

(1) Approach to the assignment:

- the consultant's understanding of the problem and of the objectives to be achieved (as set out in the terms of reference; possibly with comments on the terms and suggestions for a more effective approach than originally considered by the client);
- the assignment strategy: how to tackle the job to achieve best results;
- organization, method and scheduling of work proposed (including data on amount of work required, sequencing of operations, flow-chart diagrams, etc.;
- suggested use of special methodologies and systems (including proprietary systems) to be applied by the consultant in needs assessment, problem identification, systems design, operations scheduling, etc.;
- the client's participation in the assignment (extent, form, arrangements) as suggested and/or required by the consultant;
- impact on current operations;
- learning, financial and other benefits to the client (short-term and long-term).

(2) Staffing and backstopping:

- structure, organization and management of the team proposed;
- curriculum vitae of the team members;
- names and background (possibly curriculum vitae) of supervisors (partners, managers) responsible for the assignment in the firm's management;
- the consulting firm's technical and other facilities (e.g. local branch offices, computing services, data banks) available for technical and logistic backstopping of the project;
- suggested subcontracts to other consultants and professional firms (including local consultants or special technical services), with adequate information on these subcontractors.

(3) Profile and background of the firm:

- information on the consultant, giving the overall profile of the firm, but stressing relevant information demonstrating competence and resources needed for the given assignment;
- information on the consultant's potential to help the client beyond the scope and after the completion of the assignment.

(4) Fees and other terms:
(A wide range of points will have to be covered in this section, especially in international consulting. The most important ones are listed below).

- fee formula applied and fees to be charged (possibly a whole assignment budget);

- reimbursable expenses not included in fees;

- billing procedure;

- payment arrangements (including advance payments, deposits, letters of credit or other financial arrangements suggested to the client);

- currency of payment;

- administration and logistic support to be provided by client (office space, secretarial service, local transport, translation, interpretation, communication facilities, etc.);

- information on sales and income taxes;

- price adjustment conditions and procedures;

- conditions and procedure for early termination;

- professional and other liability; insurance coverage;

- copyright;

- governing law;

- arbitration;

- contact persons and authorized signatures.

Step 6 – Evaluation of proposals

The purpose of proposal evaluation is to identify the consultant who is best qualified for the assignment. The proposals submitted by the candidates will be carefully studied, screened, compared and assessed according to criteria which were communicated to the candidates in the letter of invitation.

The clarity of the criteria used cannot be overemphasized. In addition to being examined by the members of a selection panel or board, proposals for important and complex assignments will normally be studied and assessed by a number of managers and specialists in a client organization. Proposals for assignments funded by development bank loans or bilateral aid grants may be examined by several people in a bank or aid agency. These people should be able to refer to a few clearly spelled-out criteria in giving their subjective opinions. They should be aware of the relative importance attached to these criteria and to various sections in the consultants' proposals. In particular, it must be made clear whether price is a selection criterion and, if it is, at what stage and in what way it should be used in the selection process. Individuals involved in the evaluation of proposals should be properly briefed and should possibly hold a meeting to avoid divergencies due to the lack of communication or different subjective interpretations of various criteria.

Initial screening

It may be useful to start evaluation by rough initial screening. If many proposals were received, initial screening will identify proposals that are clearly unsuitable and can be eliminated before proceeding to detailed examination. The reasons can be various:

○   the consultant has no background and competence in the technical area or sector of the assignment;

○   the assignment is too big and complex for the consulting firm;

○   the consultant has not really prepared a proposal but only provided standard information and publicity material, or described routine techniques used for other clients;

○   the consultant has ignored the format of the submission or failed to provide essential information, thus making comparison with other proposals impossible or difficult;

○   the price is out of proportion to the client's budget estimate and to the price quotations provided by most candidates.

Obviously, the risk of receiving unsuitable proposals will be reduced by good work at the short-listing stage and by drafting precise and complete terms of reference and letters of invitation. However, the nature and novelty of the job and various other factors may cause misunderstandings and serious differences in perceptions of what is to be undertaken and what the end product should be. Therefore even a short-listed and fully competent consultant may come up with a proposal that misses the point completely. True enough, he had the possibility to visit the client organization when working on the proposal, but some consultants cannot use this opportunity owing to shortage of time or other reasons.

Initial screening may identify instances of unsuitable proposals presented by excellent consulting firms regarded as serious candidates. If the procedure and the time constraints permit it, the client may decide to go back to these consultants, asking them to rework the proposals rapidly so that they might stand a chance in the evaluation. This, however, is not permitted in some procedures.

Evaluating the consultant's approach

Proposal evaluation will be looking at the main sections of the assignment proposal as described above: proposed assignment approach (design, concept); staffing and backstopping; profile and background of the firm; and fees and other terms of the assignment.

The consultant's approach to the assignment is generally regarded as the principal criterion in assessing consulting proposals. The proposal must give a clear picture of this approach, bearing in mind that at the proposal stage everything cannot be said: solutions have yet to be found during the assignment and if the consultant anticipates some of them, he cannot reveal everything at this stage. Yet the consultant's proposal should be complete and explicit enough to demonstrate:

o   understanding of the client's problems, needs and constraints;

o   originality and novelty of the approach taken;

o   scope of the job and the requirements of the client organization;

o   short-term and long-term benefits;

o   the risks involved.

As a rule, the consultant's approach will reveal if he is a real expert in the field of the assignment, fully aware of the state of the art and informed about sources of expertise and various options that can be considered. It will also demonstrate the mastery of an effective consulting approach in outlining the problem-solving and change management methodology suited to the given assignment, including ways and methods that maximize the client's participation and learning.

Evaluating staffing and backstopping

In assessing the staffing and backstopping section, the client will be judging the size, composition and organization of the assignment team as well as the role played by the consulting firm in briefing, backstopping and controlling its team and liaising directly with the management of the client organization.

This requires several comments. Consulting firms use senior staff – the firm's owners, partners and managers – for marketing and negotiating assignments. In addition, the assignment proposal may be the result of the conceptual work of a very experienced consultant, maybe the firm's best specialist in proposal writing. The consultants proposed for the execution of the assignment may be different, often more junior, members of the firm. If the proposal comes from a solid and reputable consulting firm, it is likely that the staff proposed will be technically competent. However, you will want to be sure that the personalities of the operating consultants will match personalities in your organization. Therefore you may decide to interview the proposed team members, in particular the team leader and others playing the main roles and supposed to spend a longer time with your organization. There will be no need to interview highly specialized consultants brought in for short technical interventions.

Another important question concerns the relationship between the operating team and the consulting firm. Are they proposing to send you a team and leave it to get on with the job (this may be a cheaper solution) or will the firm be able to support and manage its team in order to ensure the best results, using the resources and know-how of the whole firm, not only of one of its many operating teams?

Evaluating the consultant's background

The profile and background of the firm may have been carefully researched when you were preparing the short-list. However, the consulting industry changes rapidly and the assignment proposal may include new useful information on the firm. Unfortunately, most consulting firms pay little attention to this section and provide standard information only. Often they do not write the section but enclose printed brochures and publicity material. You can avoid this by requesting selective information relevant to your assignment, stressing that you are keen to obtain information on new areas in development, organizational changes in the firm, alliances with other professional firms, shifts in geographic focus, recent performance figures, problems faced by the management, and so on. The consultant should be encouraged to be candid in submitting information on his firm to important clients and to reveal openly what they will find out anyway, sooner or later, from the media.

Rating

Some clients find it helpful to use a rating scheme in comparing proposals from several consultants. Every member of the selection panel makes an independent rating of each proposal; these individual ratings are compared and discussed, and an average rating is calculated.

For example, the rating scheme may establish that the three technical criteria used in rating will be those reviewed above, namely assignment approach, staffing and backstopping, and profile and background of the consulting firm. Each criterion is to be rated, using a scale of 1 to 100, with a pass grade of, say, 60. The acceptable ratings will range from 60 to 100.

Furthermore, each criterion to be rated is assigned a weight in accordance with its importance. Different weights may apply to different sorts of assignment. For example, for preinvestment studies, the World Bank suggests assigning 25 to 40 per cent to the work plan (approach to assignment), 40 to 60 per cent to key staff proposed and 10 to 20 per cent to the firm's general experience. The weight assigned to the firm's background tends to be relatively low. This background should be fully reflected in the quality of the assignment design and work plan, as well as the staff proposed. It would be of little use to have a poorly designed and staffed proposal from a highly reputable firm.

Table 4.4. Consultant rating form

Consultant	Criteria			
	A	**B**	**C**	
	Assignment design (weight = 0.40)	Staffing, backstopping (weight = 0.40)	Firm background (weight = 0.20)	Summary
	1-100 Weight Total	1-100 Weight Total	1-100 Weight Total	Total A-C
1 SANTAN	70 0.40 28	80 0.40 32	90 0.20 18	78
2 CG Consult	90 0.40 36	60 0.40 24	90 0.20 18	78
3 Pearson	70 0.40 28	50 0.40 20	90 0.20 18	66
4 etc.	0.40	0.40	0.20	
5	0.40	0.40	0.20	

An example of rating is given in table 4.4. Of the three firms listed, No. 3 has not passed the limit of 60 points in the staffing section and will be eliminated. Nos. 1 and 2 have equal total ratings, but considerable differences between the assignment design and staffing sections. Further qualitative analysis will be required.

Rating can be helpful, but it is of course subjective even if objectivity is increased by using several experienced and properly briefed evaluators. Rating should never be used to make a choice mechanically without further discussion and analysis. Simple arithmetic cannot replace managerial judgement.

Evaluating the price

As regards the role of price in evaluating proposals received from different consultants, clients have several possibilities.

The client may decide that the price will play no role in selection. The reason may be that the assignment is highly complex and exceptionally demanding on expertise, but its size and cost will be relatively small in comparison with the problem at hand, and the risk of losses, or missed opportunities, from a poorly executed job. In management consulting, this may concern critical strategy and restructuring decisions affecting the future of the business. Other examples can be multi-sectoral feasibility studies, or opinion on choices among comparable investment alternatives. If the short-list was confined to excellent professional firms whose fee structure is known, it can be assumed that the total price will be correct.

In most assignments it is not only possible, but desirable, to give consideration to the price proposed in addition to examining technical and staffing aspects of the proposal.

To make sure that the evaluators are not unduly influenced by the price proposed before they have examined the technical and staffing aspects of the proposal, some agencies recommend a two-stage procedure where technical and price proposals are submitted separately in sealed envelopes, or where price proposals are submitted at a later stage. In both cases the technical evaluation is completed before the prices proposed are examined; only technically suitable proposals are taken into consideration.

There are many approaches to the evaluation of the price of a proposal. However, the following practices prevail:

o   choosing the proposal with the lowest price. This is acceptable if the technical choice is made rigorously and the technical difference between the proposals is small. Some agencies regard this approach as straight price competition and do not recommend it;

o   choosing the lowest-priced proposal among the two or three proposals judged to be the best from the technical viewpoint;

o   using a rating formula which, in addition to the factors mentioned above, gives some weight to the price factor: this would be 30 per cent at most, but for complex assignments it would normally not exceed 10-15 per cent;

o   examining in considerable depth and detail the price of each technically eligible proposal without proceeding to any rating, and using subjective judgement to designate the best proposal using a combination of technical and price criteria.

It cannot be overstressed that the mechanical comparison of the total prices is not an adequate or appropriate way of rating consulting proposals. No rating scale can replace analysis and judgement in evaluating and selecting professional services. A strict and rigid application of straightforward rules may simplify the life of the decision-makers in the short run and protect them against accusations of favouritism, but the ultimate result can be a substandard outcome of the consultancy.

For example, if two short-listed firms of comparable reputation and experience, known for charging very similar fees, differ in their lump-sum price quotations for your assignment by more than 10-15 per cent, you should find out why before awarding the contract, even if it means that you have to re-examine the technical proposals after having seen their pricing. If the basic per diem rate normally applied by these firms is the same, price differences may mean that the cheaper firm:

o   is offering a special discount to get the job;

o   does not propose to do work that your staff can do;

o   suggests using more junior and less costly staff;

o   may have a computer programme that will save time;

o   will incur lower travel expenses;

o   views your assignment as less risky;

o   has a totally different approach to your problem.

There could be quite a few other reasons. Technical and price factors are closely interlinked and comparing prices without analysing and understanding the causes of the differences is not an effective approach to selecting consultants. To help you in this task, Chapter 5 will provide a detailed overview of current fee-setting and billing practices used by management and other consultants.

In addition to price, the evaluation will also examine other terms proposed, such as the schedule and conditions of payment. Points that should be reviewed with the consultant during negotiation will be noted. It may also be appropriate to ask the consultants to provide further explanations of terms that look unusual by the client's standards.

At the end of the evaluation phase the selection panel meets to discuss and approve the choices made. The usual practice is to discard proposals that should not be considered under any circumstances, and to rank the eligible proposals. The choice is provisional; definitive approval is to be given after contract negotiations.

Step 7 – Contract negotiation

In most procedures for consultant selection there is a provision for negotiation with the consultant whose proposal has received the best ratings. Should these negotiations fail, the second consultant is invited, and so on.

The negotiations are used to clarify all technical, staffing, administrative, legal and financial aspects of the proposal before making a final decision on the choice and preparing the consulting contract for signature.

The client uses this opportunity to comment on the proposal and suggest improvements and savings. As the client's panel has studied all proposals received, nothing can prevent the client from being inspired by information and ideas found in other proposals, and using them to improve the winning proposal. This is the risk that consultants take when submitting assignment proposals. The consultant invited to negotiations may be able to suggest improvements and savings as well. At this point he is likely to know the client organization better and may even have done some further thinking on how to improve the proposal. This is an ideal occasion for presenting these improvements to the client. Many consultants keep something "up their sleeve" for the negotiations, to demonstrate flexibility and good will in finalizing the proposal in collaboration with the client.

Certain negotiation practices are regarded as unethical, however. Proposals that will not be selected should not be handed over to the best candidate with the request to study them and exploit all useful ideas in finalizing his own proposal. It is unprofessional, and forbidden by some procedures, to give a technically superior proposal to a consultant who offered the lowest price, with a promise that he will get the contract if he maintains the price but copies the best proposal.

It is up to the client to decide how to treat price in negotiations. Generally speaking, if there is negotiation, price should be one of the topics. In some cases the existing guidelines directly encourage the clients to negotiate price. "Consulting firms are highly commercial and expect bargaining. They will normally offer discounts which can be increased in negotiation", advise the guidelines prepared by the Treasury in the United Kingdom.[1]

There are business cultures where every price quotation is regarded as negotiable and a bargaining ritual as a normal and inevitable part of a healthy business deal. If this is your culture, you should not hesitate to negotiate the price – the consultants will be well aware of your traditions and habits. However, the objectives and limits of price negotiation should be carefully reviewed before meeting the consultants. The problem with price is that it reflects a host of factors: the design, structure and staffing of the assignment, the fee formula and the fee level.

In reviewing the design, structure and staffing of the assignment, the negotiations will also look into price implications of the changes proposed and agreed to. As already stressed, major savings can often be achieved by training the client's own staff and involving them in the assignment. On the other hand, the consultant should not be pressed to assign junior staff to jobs which clearly require seasoned professionals.

The fee formula ought to be reviewed in necessary detail. The consultant should explain why he has chosen a certain fee formula, what will be included in the fee, and what will be charged as an extra or a billable expense. If the fee formula is one with which the client has no previous experience, a careful explanation of underlying assumptions by the consultant is necessary. The fee level can be negotiated if the consultant has provided fee rates per unit of time or if the client was able to make comparisons with the fees charged by other consultants for similar assignments. If the fee rates exceed the normally practised rates, the consultant can be asked for reasons.

In summary, an analytical and business-like approach to price negotiations is more professional and efficient. Yet some clients prefer global bargaining, hoping to reduce the price quoted by pressing the consultant "to make an effort".

If the consultant expects this sort of global negotiation it is quite likely that he has built a provision for a 10-15 per cent price reduction into his quotation. He may be pleased to adjust the price and everybody will be happy. Things will be more complicated and relations may get tense if the price quoted was absolutely correct and any reduction will put the consultant in difficulties. If he needs and wants the job, he will probably cede to the client's pressure and reduce the price below a normal level, hoping that he will manage somehow or see later what price adjustment may be feasible. This, however, is not a good start to a professional relationship. The consultant will sign the contract reluctantly and with a feeling of bitterness that will affect future relationships.

Generally speaking, contract negotiation is part of a consultant-client relationship and errors made at this stage will spoil the future rapport. Therefore the negotiations should be highly technical but relaxed, demonstrating to the consultant that he does not have to hide anything and that he already enjoys the client's confidence. This is a start of a long collaboration in which the partners will have to rely on each other and help each other in hundreds of work situations. Therefore the overriding question is: Are we conducting negotiations in order to understand each other better and have a fair contract to facilitate our collaboration, or do we suspect that the other partner is trying to cheat us, in which case the main purpose of the contract will be to protect us against any such attempt? It cannot be overemphasized that if the suspicions and misgivings are strong on the client's side, it may be better to decide not to sign the contract and turn to another consultant, even at this stage of the selection procedure.

In negotiations, agreement has to be reached, and properly recorded, on all points discussed. Therefore negotiators for both the consultant's and the client's side must be well prepared and fully mandated to take decisions, or must be able to seek approval from their management during negotiations.

If important and numerous changes are agreed upon, and if the consultant agrees to do more work on the design and planning of the assignment, the whole proposal may have to be redrafted and resubmitted following the negotiations, and to be rechecked by the client.

Step 8 – Selection

If contract negotiations have been successfully completed, nothing should prevent the client from rapidly making a final decision on the choice. The decision will be made by the selection board, or by the authorized manager on the selection board's recommendations.

It is good practice to inform the winner about the decision as soon as possible. If the assignment can start immediately, but the formalities involved in finalizing and signing the contract are expected to take some time, it may be possible to give the consultant an interim letter of appointment specifying what is to be done until the final contract is signed.

Unsuccessful candidates should be given a frank assessment of why they could not be chosen. Consultants who were not chosen despite their competence and well-prepared proposals should be told that their names will be kept on the client's roster and encouraged to keep the client informed about developments in their professional practice, services and products.

Step 9 – Contract finalization and signature

Chapter 6 will discuss consulting contracts in considerable detail. It will show that various forms of contract may be technically and legally acceptable and you will have to agree with the consultant on the preferred form. Either the consultant or the client may be able to provide a standard or model form of contract, which could be used as such or with modifications. As a rule, consultants realise that certain clients prefer or may be obliged to use a particular form of contract, and therefore they are flexible as regards the choice of the form, provided that the terms are acceptable to them. The text of the contract can be drafted either by the consultant or by the client. In any event, it is understood that both the client and the consultant will seek advice from their lawyers.

The signature of the contract can be done by a simple exchange of letters. Signing a major contract document may be worth a small ceremony, which also creates an opportunity for a meeting of managers from the consulting and the client organizations. A public announcement of the contract and a press release may be useful if the contract is important enough; a public announcement of major contracts may even be mandatory in some consultant selection procedures.

4.2. Special variants of the selection procedure

Consulting financed by funds borrowed from development banks

In the developing countries, many investment, structural adjustment and other projects are financed by loans granted by the World Bank or another development bank. Most of these projects include the use of consultants for feasibility studies, project design and supervision, management advice, management training and development, and other purposes. In these cases the procedure used to identify, select and employ consultants has to comply with the guidelines issued by the bank that provides the funds.

Considerable work on defining suitable procedures has been done by the World Bank, which has taken the lead in promoting good international practice in using consultants. The Bank provides its borrowers with concise guidelines for the use of consultants.[2] These guidelines are more than suggestions for good practice – if they are not observed, the borrower will face difficulties in getting the funds released and the project might even be cancelled.

The procedure to be applied in a specific project is chosen in consensus with the World Bank. Furthermore, the Bank plays several roles in the selection process in addition to the borrower and has to be consulted on important decisions such as the terms of reference, the short-list of consultants, the choice of consultant, the price to be paid and the contract to be signed. The Bank may even directly carry out certain operations required by the procedures, such as drafting the TOR, if the client does not feel competent to do so. However, the World Bank encourages the borrowers to develop the competencies needed for acting as clients in choosing and using consultants, and to become less dependent on the advice and control provided by the Bank.

To promote national self-reliance and the development of local professional consultants, and to reduce project costs, the Bank encourages the use of local consultants for jobs that do not require the competence of foreign consulting firms. Alternatively, the terms of reference may stipulate that proposals involving cooperative arrangements among consultants from developed and developing countries will be given priority.

Consulting financed by various assistance grants and loans

In a similar vein, many consultancies are financed from grants and loans provided by bilateral or multilateral aid programmes. Here too, every agency will have its own procedure, described in more or less detailed guidelines and manuals.

In some cases the acceptance of aid implies that only consultants having the nationality of a donor country, a given group of countries if aid is granted by a regional economic community (such as the EC), and, possibly, of the recipient country, are eligible for assignments financed from resources thus provided.

If you are a client who will be choosing a consultant under a tied aid arrangement, you should be aware of the criteria to be applied. The obligation to choose a consultant from a donor country may be no real constraint if the professional service sector of that country is large, competent and diversified enough to allow for choice and competition. Yet, there are two risks:

o The perspective and experience of the consultant from the donor country may be limited to the management, business and administrative know-how of his country. Is this what you want and are prepared to accept as a client?

o The donor agency may assume a major role in consultant selection, thus limiting the client's role and responsibility. True enough, the aid beneficiary will normally be consulted on the choice of the consultant and will have the right to reject a consultant regarded as unsuitable, but this may be a delicate matter in some cases. Operations such as drafting terms of reference, short-listing consultants or preparing and signing contracts, may be strongly influenced by the donor agency.

In such a context the roles of the key players in the consultant-client relationships tend to become blurred. This is no longer a bipartite but a complex tripartite relationship, which has to be handled with tact and caution:

o the principal user and client shares his rights and responsibilities with the donor agency;

o the donor agency is in a dual and often ambiguous role, acting as a client's representative in dealing with the consultant and as a supplier of consulting services in dealing with the client (and speaking on behalf of the consultant);

o the consultant has two clients and his loyalty is divided between them; if the whole loyalty goes to one client, the other client will obviously not be happy about it.

Subsidized small business consulting schemes

In several countries, small and medium-sized firms can apply for grants or subsidies in using consultants for defined purposes, such as assignments in support of new enterprise or job creation, quality improvement, business planning or export promotion. Such schemes currently exist in Germany, Ireland, Singapore, the United Kingdom and other countries.

To be entitled to the subsidy, the potential client has to contact a small business development agency and follow a particular procedure. There may be a list of consultants among whom he has to choose. The assignment proposals, or the reports on the work accomplished and results obtained, may have to be submitted to an authorising body for approval. Free assistance may be available or may have to be used for defining the most appropriate form of consultancy. In most cases the subsidy amounts to some 50 per cent of the cost of the assignment but there is an upper limit. Also, the regulations may fix the maximum daily rate payable to the consultant and other conditions.

4.3. Problems with formal selection procedures

In introducing this chapter we have mentioned the main reasons justifying the use of selection procedures. The reader should also be aware of some inconveniences of formal procedures.

High cost

The procedure can be quite costly to the client, who has to prepare and distribute voluminous documents, deal with a number of candidates, examine a great amount of technical and other documentation submitted by the consultants, hold numerous meetings and so on. On the other hand, many consultants have to do the same work in preparing proposals, but only one will get the contract. This increases the costs and the consultants will reflect this in their fees, or ask the client to reimburse directly some expenses connected with proposal preparation and discussion.

Length of procedure

A correctly applied procedure takes several months even if the job should be started urgently. Advantages of objective selection should be compared with the benefits that could be obtained thanks to prompt action.

Rigidity of procedure

It may happen that there is one excellent candidate, ready to start the job, but the procedure must be followed, thus losing time, doing unnecessary work and maybe even losing the excellent candidate who is not willing to wait for an uncertain result of a rigid selection procedure. A rigid application of the rule that the lowest bidder must be awarded the contract often has the consequence that more suitable candidates are rejected and the assignment clearly will not be in the best hands.

Barriers to participative and collaborative consulting

Selection procedures include rules and practices that make the establishment of a collaborative consultant-client relationship and the client's participation in the design of the project more difficult than less formal ways of identifying and recruiting consultants. Interaction between client and consultant personnel during the various stages of selection may even be regarded as an attempt to influence the client and resented by the selection board.

Simplified and exceptional procedures

To speed up consultant selection and correct some deficiencies of rigidly applied procedures, most consultant selection guidelines authorise certain exceptions. A common exception concerns small consulting projects, say up to US$ 70,000 - US$ 100,000. For these contracts, consultants can be selected without requesting and evaluating proposals from several candidates. Thus, it may be possible to avoid a cumbersome procedure by making the assignment smaller, or by dividing one assignment into two or three.

Some procedures admit direct selection even for larger assignments, if a long-term working contact has been established with a consultant who is known to the client organization and has rendered excellent services to it. Normally, however, a decision to proceed by direct selection has to be submitted for approval with detailed justification and a request to waive the procedure.

---

[1] HM Treasury, United Kingdom: *Seeking help from management consultants* (London, HMSO, 1990).

[2] World Bank: *Guidelines for the use of consultants by World Bank borrowers and by the World Bank as executing agency* (Washington, DC, August 1981).

ON CONSULTING FEES

5

In this chapter, you will learn about the costing, fee-setting and billing practices that prevail in today's consulting. You appreciate that consultants are in business as you are, and must be properly remunerated for their services. But what is "proper" remuneration? You might have heard that, within the same country and sector, the difference between the fees charged by the cheapest and the most expensive consultants may be 1:10, and even more. How can one explain this difference? You may have doubts about the fairness of the fees charged by your consultant. How does he arrive at his particular figure?

There should be no misunderstanding between the client and the consultant, and no feeling of uncertainty on the client's side, as regards consultant· fee levels and practices. You must be convinced that the fee is fair and that you will be getting value for your money. You should not use a consultant whom you regard as too expensive. Such a suspicion would spoil your relationship and could make your collaboration with the consultant very difficult. If your experience with using consultants is limited, you should feel free to ask your consultant for a detailed explanation of the fee proposed. A real professional has nothing to hide and will not be offended by your questions. On the contrary, it will give him an opportunity to explain his business concerns and justify the value of the services that you will be getting. Your relationship will become more transparent and more sincere.

5.1. How consultants calculate fees

The basic formula

The basic formula for establishing consulting fees is simple. Let us take an example of a sole and self-employed practitioner who does consulting for a living as a full-time occupation. His earnings from all clients served in a particular period must be sufficiently high to provide for his personal income or salary, overhead and similar expenses, taxes to be paid, and some profit. If, for example, the annual salary should be US$ 75,000 and the overhead expenses also US$ 75,000, and the gross profit at 20 per cent amounts to US$ 30,000, our consultant must be able to earn US$ 180,000 from fees charged to the clients.

Chargeable services

To collect US$ 180,000, the consultant must sell and deliver services for which he can charge this amount. These are the so-called "chargeable services", performed for and billed to particular clients. As one of these clients, you want to know exactly what is being charged to you and why. For example, if the consultant will travel to your office by car and needs five hours' driving each way, but will do, during the same trip, two days of work for you and three days for another client who is your neighbour, who will be charged for the time spent on travelling? It is good to know that some consultants charge a full rate for the time spent on travelling, some charge a reduced rate and others do not charge at all, in particular if the travel is short. In your case, a reduced rate may be appropriate. But you will probably expect the consultant to split the cost of travel time between you and your neighbour, and inform both of you about the arrangement.

Things can get complicated if several members of a consulting firm work for you in a complex assignment that involves many trips, supervision and control visits by the firm's management, and various other technical and logistic support operations. Here again, you will expect from your consultant a clear definition and justification of the supervisory and support work to be charged to you directly because the consulting firm considers it to be a part of the assignment done for you.

Services that are not directly chargeable

General management and administration of a consulting firm, and marketing and promotional activities, as well as R & D and staff training, are activities that are not related to a particular client assignment. Therefore they are not directly chargeable to individual clients. The same applies to annual leave, time lost through sickness and for various other reasons, including time lost due to a shortage of clients or to poor management of the firm.

The cost of the time spent on services and activities that are not directly chargeable will be spread over all clients through the overhead charges. The cost of the time lost or wasted due to the consulting firm's inefficient marketing or management, or due to low demand for the consultant's services, will also be spread over all clients, or may have to be treated as a loss.

A daily rate

Most consultants, as indeed other professionals such as lawyers or accountants, use one working day as a basic time unit for calculating fees. In our example, the consultant has to collect US$ 180,000 in one year, but in how many working days (or other units such as months) of chargeable time?

Every consulting firm has its own chargeable time budget, and there are different budgets for different categories of consultants, since all of them cannot spend the same amount of time working directly for clients. This budget is established by deducting, from the total number of working days in a calendar year, the days spent on activities for which the clients cannot be directly charged, as well as the days lost for any reasons, subjective or objective.

In professional services, it is unthinkable to charge directly for 100 per cent of theoretical working time. As a rule, in efficiently run consulting firms the time utilization (days actually chargeable: days available) attains some 80-90 per cent for operating staff, 60-70 per cent for senior staff involved in supervision and marketing, and 0-50 per cent for higher management staff. The firm's management may do no chargeable work for individual clients, although many partners with important management and practice-promotion and marketing responsibilities are also keen to work directly for clients from time to time.

These considerations explain the fee rate that the consultant quotes to you. He needs to earn US$ 180,000, while his annual budget of chargeable time is, say, 180 days. This will leave some 40 days for marketing, training, attending professional meetings and writing articles, and another 40 days for leave, public holidays and reserve against sickness. Thus, the consultant's daily fee must be at least US$ 1,000.

Some clients would compare this figure with the monthly salaries of their managerial and specialist staff, and find it exorbitant. This is an unfair and unrealistic approach. Remember, our consultant's real monthly income is US$ 75,000 ÷ 12 = US$ 6,250 without profit and US$ 8,750 with profit. He will be able to charge for 15 days a month, but he will spend US$ 6,250 on various overhead charges and expenses.

There are consultants who charge higher fees and earn more money. As a client, you will want to know why this is so. Maybe you could get the same service for a lower price. But it would be futile to think that high-level professional advisers can work for low fees!

5.2. Information on fee levels

To avoid any suspicion and misunderstanding due to lack of information, both clients and consultants should make enough effort to exchange and analyse information on fee practices and be aware of the forces that tend to push the fee levels upwards. Unfortunately, there is a general shortage of information on fee levels practised at the market for professional services. On the consultants' side, some (but not all) consulting associations and institutes produce statistical information on fee practices, or issue guidelines concerning suggested fee levels. Such information is available to both consultants and clients. On the clients' side, business partners and friends may share information on fees paid to consultants, but trade and employers' associations could certainly do more to help their members in getting and sharing reliable information on consulting and other professional service fees.

For obvious reasons, consulting fees will be higher in high-income and high-cost industrialized countries, such as the United States or Switzerland. For example, according to an ACME survey, typical hourly billing rates in the United States were in 1992 as shown in table 5.1. A median fee rate applied by American management consultants in 1989 was about US$ 1,000 per day, with average fee levels in financial management some 10 per cent higher than in production and 25 per cent higher than in personnel management. To quote another example, the ASCO in Switzerland issued guidelines suggesting hourly fees as indicated in table 5.2.

Table 5.1. Standard hourly billing rates in the United States in 1992 (in US$)

Level of consultant	All responding firms	Size of professional staff in firm			
		Less than 15	15 - 50	51 - 150	151 or more
Research associate	63	65	68	58	60
Operating consultant	112	112	121	125	100
Senior consultant	150	140	153	165	141
Senior partner or equivalent	200	200	220	200	250

Table 5.2. Hourly fee rates suggested by ASCO in 1992 (in Swiss francs)

Consultant's qualification	Duration and nature of assignment		
	A few days/ advice to top management	Several weeks/ development of concepts	Several weeks/ detailed analysis and operations
Expert in methodology and strategy	450	300	300
Specialist in particular technical fields	300	270	240
Independent collaborator		240	180
Assistant		150	120

In the United Kingdom, the 1991 standard daily fee levels practised by management consultants were as follows: solo practitioner, £300-500; small consulting firm, £400-600; medium-sized consultancy (10-50 consultants), £600 and more; large firm, £750 and more. With the growing globalization of the economy and internationalization of consulting, the fees tend to level off. However, in lower-income countries the services of most high-level professionals from high-income countries can be too expensive by local standards, and many local firms could hardly afford to pay these fees. The solution is in the development of a local consulting profession, so that it could provide services of satisfying quality for locally acceptable prices.

5.3. Fee-setting practices

Management consultants use several methods of fee-setting and billing, and the range of these methods tends to grow. In proposing an assignment, your consultant may suggest two or more alternative methods, and you should be able to assess their advantages and shortcomings. Alternatively, you may have to compare proposals from consultants using different fee-setting methods. The method chosen should be acceptable to both the consultant and the client, and suitable for the job to be done.

Time-based fee

Most consultants prefer time-based fees, i.e. charging the client for the time actually worked at the assignments. The time unit used can be an hour (more and more frequent, in particular in short assignments), a day (the principal method), a week or a month (in longer assignments, e.g. in technical assistance projects in developing countries). The rationale behind the fee rate used was explained in previous sections. Thus, a consulting firm may propose to charge several different rates, depending on the sort and level of expertise required in an assignment.

To many consultants, charging the client for the time actually worked and the level of expertise actually provided is the best and only professionally acceptable method of billing. They hold the view that the very nature of consulting makes it impossible to plan the volume and results of an assignment with absolute precision, and that the client's participation and consultant-client collaboration are encouraged if the client pays the consultant for the time used in working together.

However, both consultants and clients agree that time-based rates have the following three shortcomings:

- the lack of predictability ("the meter keeps running and you don't know what the ceiling is");

- the absence of risk-sharing between the consultant and the client (there is no risk to the consultant, since he will be paid anyhow, whatever the progress and the results of the assignment);

- the lack of any incentive to work more efficiently (occasionally you may even suspect that your consultant is working slowly and doing unnecessary things in order to stay longer and earn more money from you).

These shortcomings of time-based contracts can be mitigated by careful time planning, regular monitoring and your active participation in the work done by the consultant. However, you should be convinced that you have made the best possible choice and trust your consultant not only for his integrity, but also for his capability to work effectively and efficiently.

Flat (lump-sum) fee

If the consultant is recruited for a job that can be relatively well analysed, defined and assessed, it may be possible and appropriate to apply a flat or lump-sum fee. In this case the client will know in advance how much the whole assignment will cost. The consultant will know that he will not receive the fee, or its considerable portion, if the job defined in the contract is not completed.

The use of flat fees or fixed-price contracts has become increasingly popular in recent years. The promoters of this fee-setting and billing technique argue that by working for a flat fee the consultant takes most of the risk involved. He is encouraged to be results oriented and efficiency minded and avoid cost overruns. He knows that if he has to work overtime he will not be able to charge additional fees. This makes life easier for the client and actually helps to sell more consulting work to those clients who do not like uncertainty and risk in recruiting professional advisers. Public sector clients often have a fixed budget for a particular consulting project and are happy if the consultant commits himself to remain within this budget's limits.

A consultant would normally base his flat-fee proposal on a detailed assessment of the time required by the assignment. He will tend to be more precise and more meticulous in looking at details and in defining the client's inputs in the assignment in terms of staff time and competence, documentation, administrative support, assignment control meetings with the consultant, and the like. Quite often, the consultant will be proposing to work for a flat-fee because he has done similar jobs for other clients and knows how long they would normally take. However, the consultant is taking a risk and has to protect himself against unforeseen events, and will also wish to build in some incentive for himself. Therefore a flat fee may include a hidden contingency provision and a higher profit margin than in the case of time-based contracts.

If the consultant achieves the agreed technical results and meets the deadlines, there should be satisfaction on both sides. The consultant may even have spent less time and achieved a handsome profit. Nevertheless, the client might suspect that due to this fee arrangement he has ended up by paying too much, even if he is satisfied by the technical results of the assignment.

If the job is not completed as foreseen and there is a cost overrun, the consultant will make no profit and may even end up with a loss. He may have to work for free in order to complete the job. Legally there is no problem, since the consultant was well aware of this risk when signing the contract. There may be a technical and human problem, however. For example, the planned results could not be defined with absolute precision in the consulting contract, and if the results actually achieved are difficult to assess, the consultant may be tempted to deliver a job of a lower quality and argue that this is what was agreed; or he may argue that the objectives could not be met due to the client's inadequate inputs, and the like.

Therefore fixed-price contracts require careful preparation and negotiation by both the consultant and the client. They should not be used in dealing with vaguely defined and open-ended problems. Some of their drawbacks can be overcome by using the following fee arrangements:

o   a lump sum is set as an upper limit, but the actual fee will be paid on a time basis within this limit;

o   a provision is made in the contract for adjusting the total fee if this is justified by reasons that could not be foreseen when the contract was signed;

o   a provision is made for paying a special bonus to the consultant on the top of the flat fee if excellent results (in terms of quantity and quality) are achieved;

o   several consultants are invited to suggest a flat fee based on assessment of the volume of work required; the proposals received are compared and carefully analysed to arrive at a more accurate planning of the whole job.

Occasionally, a consultant who is in need of work may decide to underrate the assignment's real cost and offer to work for an unusually low flat fee to be sure that he will get the job. This is unprofessional and hazardous. It is equally hazardous for the client to accept such an offer in the belief that he is making a bargain.

Fee contingent on results

A fee contingent on results (contingent or contingency fee) will be paid only when specific results defined in the consulting contract are achieved, and the size of the fee will depend on the size of the results (profit, cost reductions, savings, etc.).

A clear advantage of this formula is its total results orientation. As the consultant knows that he will not get any fee if the assignment does not produce results, many problems involved in using time-based or flat fees will thus be avoided. The contingency fees encourage innovation, entrepreneurship and risk taking. They also exhibit serious shortcomings that limit the scope of their use in consulting:

o   it may be very difficult to agree on results that can be correctly measured;

o   the results achieved will be the client firm's results, not the consultant's results, and therefore a conflict can easily develop over the actual responsibility for these results;

o   the results can be improved by decisions and measures that create visible short-term benefit but neglect the long-term interests of the client or even lead to serious losses in the future (e.g. by neglecting maintenance or research);

o   it is not clear when to pay the consultant if the results can only be measured some time after the end of the assignment;

o   if the client company is in difficulties, or if the business climate deteriorates beyond expectations, the projected results may never be attained.

If your consultant suggests a contingency fee for a job such as a major restructuring of your business, do not accept this proposal without very careful scrutiny. It is possible that a flat fee plus special bonus would be a better arrangement for both of you. An alternative formula may be to offer the consultant some form of equity (stocks or stock options) as a bonus in addition to a per diem or flat-rate fee. The value of this equity will be affected by your company's future performance, so this is a sort of contingency fee. So far, this formula has been seldom used, but it is becoming more popular. It has been used by several American consultants doing intensive work for high-technology companies during the start-up phase, when the need for advice is very high but resources for paying consultants limited.

It is good to know that despite their apparent appeal, contingency fees have been one of the most controversial issues in management consulting. They have supporters, but most professionals continue to reject them. In management consulting they used to be banned by the professional codes of conduct. This ban has been lifted in most countries, but no professional asso-

---

ciation has been promoting their use. In 1990 the FEACO clearly stated in its new guidelines on the interpretation of the professional code of conduct that "in circumstances where a contingent fee basis might operate in a manner which could prejudice the independence of the consultants undertaking the assignment or might prove difficult to calculate in practice or might prejudice the long-term relationship with the client, it must not be used."

Percentage fee

A percentage fee is a kind of contingency fee, tied to the value of a business transaction, such as a merger, an acquisition, a real-estate closing, a joint venture, a bond issue or similar. Traditionally, real-estate agents and investment bankers have charged percentage fees for their services in these transactions. Over the last ten to 15 years management and business consultants have expanded their activities in these areas, following the fee patterns already practised by investment bankers and other agents acting as intermediaries and facilitators of major business deals. Percentage fees are common in architecture and civil engineering, where the consulting engineer's remuneration is often calculated as a percentage of the total project cost plus reimbursable direct cost.

A typical example of a percentage fee is the Lehman formula, or the 5-4-3-2-1 formula, which continues to be the standard method of structuring the intermediary's (broker's or finder's) fee in mergers and acquisitions, although a number of modifications of the basic formula are in use. The classic Lehman formula is based on the acquisition price and uses a descending percentage scale as follows:

5% of US$1 to US$1,000,000
4% of US$1,000,001 to US$2,000,000
3% of US$2,000,001 to US$3,000,000
2% of US$3,000,001 to US$4,000,000
1% of US$4,000,001 and up.

Thus, the consultant's success fee for the sale of a US$5 million company would be $(0.05+0.04+0.03+0.02+0.01) \times US\$1$ million = US$150,000. An alternative of the formula is 5 per cent of the first US$2 million, 4 per cent of the next US$2 million, and so on. Another alternative in use is 5 per cent of the first US$5 million, 2.5 per cent of the next US$10 million and 0.75 per cent of any amount in excess of US$15 million. A fixed percentage fee (1 to 3 per cent) is also practised, as well as various bonus formulas. Such a bonus would be paid in addition to the normal fee if the selling price obtained in the transaction exceeded a certain limit. The bonus can be calculated as a percentage of the whole transaction or of the part of the price in excess of the agreed amount (which is preferable).

Some consultants prefer different fee formulas to be sure to earn something even if the deal fails. For example, a retainer or per diem fee is paid, but if the deal is concluded a percentage fee is applied and the fee paid on a per diem basis is deducted from the total amount.

It is easy to see that the fees paid to investment bankers or consultants helping to prepare and negotiate important deals can be very high. However, there is a risk of failure and a lot of time is also spent on preparing and negotiating deals that never materialize. Most importantly, bringing the deal to a successful closing is a special skill for which even seasoned managers are prepared to pay a high price.

Of course, clients who regard these fees as exorbitant have always the possibility to negotiate the deals directly, without recruiting an investment banker, a management consultant or another intermediary. They may only retain the services of a lawyer for advice on the legal and contractual aspects of the operation, and in some companies even this service can be handled by their own legal departments.

Retainer fee

This fee is paid to a consultant who has a retainer arrangement with the client. As a rule, the retainer will be for a fixed number of days of the consultant's time over a period (say, two days every month over a three-year period). The consultant will apply his normal daily rate, but this rate may be slightly reduced since the retainer ensures a steady income to the consultant and saves marketing time. The client will have to pay even if he does not have enough work for the consultant.

Reimbursable expenses

The consultant's fee for an assignment can be all-inclusive. In such a case the consultant cannot ask the client for any other payments over and above the fee. It is understood that the overhead charge (which is part of the fee) includes a sufficient provision for expenses such as administrative support, or travel and communication expenses.

Small cost items, whose separate recording and billing to clients item by item would be impractical and costly, are normally treated as part of overhead costs. As regards more important expense items that are directly related to particular assignments, the normal practice is to treat them as "reimbursable" or "billable" expenses. They are billed to the client separately from the fee proper.

The reimbursable expenses include the cost of the consultant's travel, board and lodging during the assignment, long-distance communication, document reproduction, printing and delivery, purchase of special equipment and documentation, computer services, royalties and similar. These expenses can be quite high in international consulting involving a great deal of travel and other costs (they may even involve family travel if the consultant is to work on a long assignment abroad) and if costly proprietary systems are used for which the consultant charges a high fee. Therefore it is important to define clearly, before starting the assignment, what expenses will be reimbursed to the consultant. For example, will the consultant be entitled to travel first or business class? Will board and lodging be reimbursed on the basis of standard daily rates or according to expenses actually incurred? Will any upper limits be fixed for these expenses? What systems can be regarded and treated as proprietary and what fee will the client be prepared to pay for their use?

Reimbursable expenses are normally charged to clients net, without any overhead or profit charge. Some consultants or technical assistance agencies employing consultants mark up these expenses, adding a 7-15 per cent service charge to cover their administrative costs connected with handling these expenses.

5.4. Billing and payment schedules

In proposing a billing and payment schedule, the consultant has to aim to collect the fees for the work performed without undue delays, and to avoid extending free credit to the clients or their bankers. In short assignments, the client is likely to receive the bill a few weeks after the end of the assignment. In some countries it is a matter of courtesy not to issue the bill immediately after the assignment. However, a delay of three to four months may be a sign of poor administration within the consulting firm. In longer assignments clients are billed periodically (e.g. monthly) if time-based fees are used. Payments are normally due within 30 days after billing, but this period might be extended to 60 days in some international contracts.

If the consultant does not receive payment within the agreed period, the client may have a contractual obligation to pay interest on delayed payment. Conversely, there may be a provision for a discount (say 2-3 per cent) on timely payments.

If you have agreed to a flat fee, the billing and payment schedule has to be given careful consideration. You may have to make periodic partial payments. If not, the consultant will need to borrow money to run his operation and pay the staff, and this will force him to increase the flat-fee rate.

Quite often in a flat-fee assignment the consultant will propose a payment schedule that foresees a fairly important initial down-payment on signature (up to 30 per cent) before committing resources and starting operations. This is an acceptable practice, but the client must be absolutely sure that the consultant is trustworthy and his financial position solid. Otherwise it would be appropriate to require a bank guarantee or a bond in return for the receipt of an advance payment made to the consultant (see section 5.5).

In discussing billing practices and schedules with your consultant, you should insist on receiving detailed and clearly worded bills to avoid any misunderstanding. The consultant must tell you exactly what he is charging for and why. Normally in a bill you should not find any unexpected charge, for example for extra services commissioned by the consultant to a subcontractor without your agreement. Information normally provided in a bill is given in table 5.3.

Table 5.3. Information provided in a bill – Checklist

1. Bill number.
2. Period covered.
3. Services provided (listing, dates, volume of work by each consultant).
4. Fee rates and total charges.
5. Expenses billed separately from fees.
6. When payment is due.
7. How to make payment (currency, method of payment, account number).
8. Whom to contact for queries.
9. Date of expedition of the bill.
10. Name, address, telephone, telex and fax numbers of the consultant.
11. Signature and courtesy formula.

The payment of fees can be slowed down by various factors, in particular in international consulting. Even if a client promptly approves the bill received and authorizes the payment, the procedure may take three to four months owing to government bureaucracy and inefficient or purposely slow banking practices. If this can be anticipated, the consultant may request that the client arranges for the establishment of a bank deposit (revolving fund) or a letter of credit permitting the consultant to draw against the client's funds as soon as the latter has endorsed the bills received.

What will happen at the end of the assignment if you are not satisfied with the results? A flat fee is not a contingency fee, so you will not be able to request the consultant to return the money received through a partial advance payment. As a rule, you will try to negotiate a compromise, pointing out that the job has not been completed according to the contract. The compromise may imply that the consultant will have to do additional work to finish the job. Alternatively, you may suggest reducing the total fee, but the consultant is likely to accept your suggestion only if he shares the view that the result is not fully satisfactory.

The situation is different in the case of contingency fees. There is no need to make advance payments. The fee is due when the agreed results have been achieved and can be measured. This may not be possible until several months or even years after the completion of the consultancy.

A percentage fee paid to intermediaries on mergers and acquisitions is computed as a percentage of the acquisition price paid either at closing or over some period of time after closing. If payments of the price are made over time, a present value is normally computed as of the date of closing in order to arrive at a basis for calculating the fee to be paid.

5.5. Guarantees, bonds and retentions

In consulting, a client would seldom request his contractor to provide a financial guarantee of service performance. The World Bank and the consultants' associations (e.g. the International Federation of Consulting Engineers – FIDIC) advise against the use of bonds and similar guarantees which they regard as unnecessary if consultants are chosen on the basis of competence and reputation. Furthermore, as FIDIC points out, the presence or absence of bonds does not affect the legal liability of parties to a contract to conform to its provisions.[1] Yet some public sector clients have been obliged by the consultant recruitment and contracting procedure to require guarantees practised in the construction sector. Occasionally, a client may feel that the provision of a financial guarantee in the form of a bond is justified by the importance of the consulting project, the financial loss that could be caused by the consultant's failure to complete the project, or the risk taken by awarding the contract to an unknown consultant. The establishment of a bond is then a matter for the client and the consultant to consider and decide by agreement. Consultants can turn to banks and insurance companies that will issue a bank guarantee or security bond for a reasonable fee. This, however, will be an extra cost to the consultant, who most probably will try to transfer this cost to the client.

Bid bonds are requested by clients in some bidding procedures from all consultants participating in bidding to guarantee that they are serious bidders and will not withdraw in the course of the procedure. However, if the client fails to agree with the consultant on the costs or other conditions of the contract, this should not be used as a justification for calling the bond.

Advance payment bonds and bank guarantees are intended to guarantee that the consultant will perform the services for which he has been paid in advance. They are justified if the consultant is not well known to the client, the sum to be paid in advance is important, or the client has doubts about the consultant's financial health.

Performance bonds and guarantees are intended to guarantee proper performance and completion of the consultant's services. In considering their use it is essential to clearly define what is performance, when and by whom it will be measured, and whether the guarantee is really useful and necessary.

None of the guarantees described should be of the unilateral "on demand" or "on call" variety, where the client can require and obtain a payment without providing any justification.

Retentions from periodic (monthly) partial payments to the consultant are generally regarded as inappropriate, with the exception of instances where the client contests the justification of a charge (supporting documents are missing or the consultant is charging for a service that was not foreseen in the contract and not authorized by the client).

Retentions from final payments may under certain circumstances serve a useful purpose. For example, the client may retain the final payment or its part until it can be duly established that the assignment has been fully completed and all conditions of the contract met.

---

[1] *FIDIC policy statement on guarantees, bonds and retentions relating to professional services* (Aug. 1986).

ON CONSULTING CONTRACTS

6

If a consultant works for a client as an independent supplier of professional services on a commercial basis, i.e. for a fee, an agreement on the provision of these services is a contract in the legal sense of the term. The two parties have made an exchange of promises and if this exchange meets certain conditions (e.g. the subject is legal, the parties have full capacity to contract and the exchange was not made under undue influence), the contract is legally binding even if it has not been made in writing.

The purpose of this chapter is to acquaint you with current contracting practices used in consulting. Contracting is an important aspect of consulting, and therefore both clients and consultants should know how to draft and use contracts. A consulting contract is a management tool above all. Contracting permits one to define objectives, structure and plan the assignment, decide on resources, and clarify commitments in detail and with precision. Contracting encourages systematic thinking, consistency and discipline in using the services of professional advisers. It ensures continuity (e.g. if people change on the client's and the consultant's side, or if new assignments are planned and started and in some way affect the areas and activities covered by a current assignment).

Most important, the very fact that a contract is to be drafted which will be a legally enforceable document encourages the client and the consultant to give consideration to a number of points that would otherwise be ignored. It helps them to face the issue of reasonable sharing of risks and responsibilities in a joint undertaking.

If everything is in order and the assignment is progressing normally, the legal dimension of contracting is hardly noticed. The contract is used as a technical document and guideline for action. If relations start deteriorating or go wrong, the legal nature of the contract is rediscovered. All of a sudden the contract is viewed as a tool for protecting the client's or the consultant's interests against the other party and every term used in the text becomes important.

Indeed, to safeguard the contract parties' interest is an overriding function of contracting. Yet legal considerations should not be permitted to dominate the rapport of the partners in a consulting assignment. The human relationships, mutual understanding and the desire to bring a common project to a successful completion are infinitely more important. In excellent consulting assignments, there is a psychological contract between the consultant and the client, which cannot be replaced even by the finest legal document.

6.1. Forms of contract

Oral contract

An oral (parol) contract, or verbal agreement, is recognized as fully acceptable and binding by legislation in most countries. This includes contracts concerning consulting services. If a client asks a consultant "to have a quick look at the product-costing system and suggest how it can be improved" and the consultant agrees to do it, this is usually a contract even if the duration of the assignment, the depth of the study and the fee to be paid are not specified. But there is a potential risk of misunderstanding. The consultant may regard this definition of the task as a small but regular assignment. Yet the client may have in mind a preliminary investigation for which he would not be charged.

Many problems may arise even if both the client and the consultant belong to the same community and are used to the same terms of business. If consultants intervene in alien countries and cultures, the risks of misunderstanding and conflict can be tremendous.

The main problem with oral contracts is that it is extremely difficult and in some cases impossible to produce evidence concerning the purpose and terms of the contract. Even if everyone is acting in good faith, people can easily forget what was discussed and agreed; or they do not brief their collaborators clearly and completely, and there can be conflicting views on the scope, method and end result of the consultancy both within the client organization and in the consulting firm.

These and similar reasons make oral contracts unsuitable for most consulting assignments. True enough, in the history of consulting many excellent assignments were negotiated and executed without any written agreement. Even at the present time oral contracts are regarded as sufficient by some clients and consultants who know and understand each other perfectly and are able to interpret the other party's thinking, even if the consultancy was discussed casually over a telephone. However, currently the use of oral contracts tends to be limited to small and short assignments in situations where the client and the consultant know each other rather well and where no formal consultant selection procedure is used. In other cases, both clients and consultants prefer a written form of contract.

Written contract

Written contracts come in many varieties. Frequent users of consultants, in particular in the public sector, have their standard terms of contract. The FIDIC has developed a client-consultant model service agreement for consulting in engineering and recommends its general use for the purposes of pre-investment and feasibility studies, designs and administration of construction and project management, in particular if services are invited and delivered on an international basis.[1] The World Bank has issued a sample contract for consultants' services in complex time-based assignments.[2] International agencies, governments and many consulting firms also have their standard contract texts. Some consultants use standard terms of business, which can be used in drafting a contract or attached to the contract without or with modification. Then they become part of the contract.

Because of the diversity of purposes covered by contracts and of the terms of various consultancies, we have chosen not to give a model contract text in this publication. Rather than that, section 6.4 will provide a typical contract outline and comment on important contract terms, in particular in cases where international practice is not united.

Letter of agreement or intent

A complete consulting contract can be quite an elaborate document and its drafting and negotiation can take a lot of time. Therefore many clients and consultants prefer simpler legally valid forms of written contracts.

A popular and widely used way of contracting professional services is a letter of agreement (other terms used: letter of intent, of engagement, of appointment). Having received and reviewed the consultant's proposal, the client sends him a letter of agreement, confirming that the proposal is accepted (a simple endorsement by the client on a copy of the consultant's proposal would normally be sufficient). The letter may set out new conditions that modify or supplement the consultant's proposal. In this case it is the consultant who in turn replies as to whether or not he accepts these new conditions. The procedure can also be used even with large and complex assignments, if the consultant's proposal is clear and complete and does not require many modifications.

Alternatively, the letter of agreement or intent can be drafted by the client and sent to the consultant. If the consultant accepts the proposed terms of reference, he gives written agreement and the contract is made.

If several letters are exchanged in which the conditions are amended, it is useful to repeat the proposal in the last letter and have it countersigned by the other party on the copy of that letter.

Before signing any letter of agreement or intent, the client should be aware of the legal implications. The question to ask is: Are we ready and do we want to sign a legal commitment at this stage? Maybe the client intends to use the consultant and wishes to make a clear statement to this effect, but is not yet sure that he fully agrees to the course of action proposed, the size of the budget or another element of the project under consideration.

Letters of intent and similar documents are used in many business transactions, such as mergers, acquisitions or joint ventures. The same words of caution apply: do not sign any letter of intent stipulating or implying a commitment that you are not ready to make, such as agreeing to a major business transaction before all necessary investigations have been completed and the various conditions of the transaction fixed, or committing yourself not to negotiate with other parties. Should you find it useful to have a letter of intent that is not a binding legal document, a proper statement can be included in the text (such as: "this letter is a statement of intent only and is not binding on the parties").

Purchase order

Many client organizations in various countries use preprinted purchase order forms for contracting consulting services, in particular for smaller assignments that do not require long preliminary discussions and detailed proposals. The purchase order describes the services to deliver and sets out the conditions of payment. Standard conditions of contract may be reproduced on the verso of the document or attached to it. The consultant receives two copies and, if he accepts the order, signs and returns one copy to the client.

Implied contract

Whatever form of contract is chosen, the consultant or the client may either forget to specify certain terms, or may regard such a specification as unnecessary. A client may not ask for a fee quotation if he knows the fees normally charged by the consultant. The consultant knows that he will never collect the last 5 per cent of the fee if this is the normal way of doing business in the client's country. In an implied contract, the parties have not fully expressed their intentions and terms, but these can be inferred from the circumstances. An implied term can be a term that goes without saying or a term which, although unexpressed, forms part of the contract. Such terms are legally binding in most countries.

6.2. Drafting a contract

When you start preparing and negotiating a consulting assignment, it is useful to think of the form of contract that you will wish to sign with your consultant. If you have a standard form of contract, it may be useful to make it available to the short-listed consultants as an appendix to the terms of reference and the letter of invitation. In telling the consultants how they should present their proposals you would normally keep in mind the scope and terms of the contract to be signed. Either you will ask the consultant to provide information required for the contract, including his particular terms, or, if you provide your terms when soliciting proposals, you will inform the consultant that he will have to comply with certain terms if the contract is awarded to him. Generally speaking, it is advisable to structure the assignment proposal in a way that will permit its direct use in the text of the contract, or as an appendix to the contract.

The text of the contract can be prepared either by the client or by the consultant. A consultant experienced in drafting contracts can render a useful service to the client by taking care of this task, in particular if the client is willing to accept the consultant's standard terms of business. However, if a client has to comply with numerous regulations governing the use of contracts in his particular context, it is better if he drafts the contract, or provides the consultant with detailed information on the terms that will have to be observed.

You do not have to use a lawyer to draft the contract. It is even preferable if the first text is not produced by a lawyer. Consulting contracts should be drafted in clear and simple language and the typical legal jargon, which only lawyers understand, should be avoided. Furthermore, asking a lawyer to write the whole contract text may be quite costly.

Yet the contract will be a legal document and ought to be reviewed by a lawyer on both the client's and the consultant's side. In international consulting, the parties will have to choose the law to which the contract is subject and according to which it will have to be construed. Lawyers will be able to advise you on country differences, of which both the client and the consultant should be fully aware before signing. They will draw your attention to omissions and risks of which you may be unaware.

Finally, even if your lawyer tells you that you can sign the contract without any risk, it cannot be overemphasized that you should read the contract text carefully before signing. It is always possible to ask for last-minute explanations and corrections to avoid misunderstanding and future problems.

6.3. Flexibility in consulting contracts

The drafting of contract texts requires precision and thoroughness. However, the reader could object that an excessively meticulous and legalistic approach is not suitable for setting the terms of consulting assignments, which typically concern situations involving uncertainty, change, innovations and alternative courses of action that cannot be foreseen and described with precision when the contract is drafted.

Generally speaking, the nature of the assignment dictates the nature of the contract, and not vice versa. If it is impossible to produce a detailed work plan for more than six months, the contract form must not impose a detailed work plan for three years. It is in the client's and the consultant's common interest to decide what should be determined and planned in considerable detail, and where more global approaches can be used.

Flexibility can be increased, for example:

o   through periodic reviews built into the contract permitting its adjustment to changed circumstances;

o   by signing detailed contracts for shorter periods of time (e.g. for the first two phases in a five-phase project) as well as a global agreement on how the project will be pursued and detailed contracts for the next phases prepared if the job progress is satisfactory;

o   by using time-based and retainer contracts if the client wants to retain the consultant's services for the whole duration of the project, without, however, being prepared to agree on detailed objectives, work plans and budget for all project phases when signing the contract;

o   by incorporating a contingency allowance into the contract, to finance unforeseen additional work and provide for cost increases due to price adjustment (without a contingency allowance it may be extremely difficult to adjust contracts to changed circumstances, or the volume of services will have to be reduced due to cost increases).

A flexible approach to contracting also provides for contract termination before the date of completion agreed in the contract. It must be possible to terminate the contract if the client's condition has changed and the consultancy is no longer required. Other justified reasons for termination may be the consultant's poor performance, a profound conflict of personalities, the client's failure to provide the agreed inputs, changes in the client or the consulting organization that make the continuation of the assignment impossible or impractical, *force majeure* independent of the consultant's and the client's control, and so forth.

Certain practices are used to enhance contract flexibility, although they may be unauthorized by company regulations, or even illegal. Often public sector clients have recourse to such practices in good faith, to eliminate the red tape and expedite the work that needs to be done.

For example, some clients would sign a contract for one job, but ask the consultant to do another one. The reason may be that the needs have changed, but it is not practical to repeat a cumbersome selection procedure or resubmit the modified project for approval; or it is not permitted to recruit consultants for certain sorts of jobs even if they are needed and will be used for these jobs.

Inadequate fee rates approved by government authorities or international agencies force some public sector clients to pay consultants for more days than actually worked by making generous provisions for preparatory work, data collection and report writing. Many consultants agree to this practice despite the fictitious rates, to make life easier for public sector clients.

In other cases, clients sign consulting contracts although the budget allocation is obviously insufficient for the job. They do this knowing that they could not get more money in the current budgetary period, in the belief that the rest of the money will be authorized in the next period and the consultant will be able to finish the job. Quite a few times the next allocation is never authorized and the job never finished.

A variant of this approach is a "second-best" assignment design. Resources to do a fully satisfactory job are not available, so the consultant is offered a contract to do "as much as he can". For example, the fact-finding omits certain facts, the training required is reduced, only a few and not all people are trained, certain product lines are deleted from the study, and so on.

In both public and private organizations it is common practice to alter the work plan and some of the terms in the course of contract fulfilment by oral agreement, without changing the written contract or recording the agreed modification in any way. For example, the consultant is authorized orally to spend more time and resources on certain inputs than stipulated by the contract. As a result, in addition to the written contract there are one or more oral contracts on the same matter. This may create an uncontrollable situation and a real nightmare in case of a misunderstanding or conflict on what was actually agreed and authorized.

6.4. International contract outline with a commentary

The headings and subheadings used in this section correspond to section headings normally used in international consulting contracts. Therefore the reader can use this section as a commented checklist in preparing or examining a contract. We have refrained from suggesting a complete contract text. Contracts come in so many variants that this would be not only impractical but even misleading to some readers whose specific needs and conditions would not be taken into consideration. As mentioned in section 6.1, various standard or model texts of contracts are readily available.

In structuring the contract, it is possible to proceed in various ways. For example:

o   the contract is in two parts: standard conditions and conditions of particular application (FIDIC model);

o the contract is in one part combining both standard and particular conditions;

o the contract text describes the particular tasks and conditions, and the standard terms of business are included in an appendix, and so on.

Agreement preamble

The contract text normally opens with a short formula stating the decision of the contracting parties to sign a contract for the provision of consulting services. Preamble formulas are particularly common in international business and consulting, and often provide summary information on the background of the relationship, the reasons for the decision, the history of the negotiations, the sources of funds, the development objective pursued and similar. Although formally separated from the body of the contract and often regarded as pure formality or courtesy, the statement made in the preamble may have legal implications. The contents of the preamble may be used in interpreting the contract or examining the competence and mutual commitments of the parties.

Definitions

The terms used in the contract could lend themselves to various interpretations. For example, will "project" mean the services to be performed by the consultant (consulting project), or a wider set of activities pursued by the client of which the assignment is only one part? This section provides definitions for the purpose of the contract. The key terms normally defined are: project, assignment (services), client, consultant, party, agreement (contract), personnel, subcontractor, day, and so on.

Assignment description

The assignment description indicates the scope of the assignment, objectives, activities, volume of work, products and other results, work plan and timetable, approach to be taken, special work methods to be applied, and so on. The description should be as detailed and precise as possible. If the assignment is part of a wider project or technical assistance programme, this relationship should be described.

In preparing the contract, the assignment was first defined briefly in the terms of reference, then outlined in detail and commented on in the consultant's proposal and reviewed during contract negotiations. Therefore producing another, or differently structured, description would not be practical in most cases. Normally the assignment proposal prepared by the consultant and amended after negotiations would either be included in this section, or appended to the contract. Elements of the consultant's proposal which should not be included in the contract (e.g. general background information on the consulting firm) will be deleted.

Obligations of the consultant

This section includes statements of the consultant's contractual obligations in performing the assignment. There will be no need to repeat the description of technical activities made in the assignment description. However, a number of points will be covered concerning the general obligations of the consultant and the personnel (staff) appointed to the assignment. Although some of the points may be sufficiently covered in the general codes of conduct and ethics of the profession, many clients find it appropriate to include specific statements (sometimes more detailed and adapted to the client's conditions) in the text of the contract.

Additional services

Under what circumstances the consultant is to provide services not foreseen in the contract, and how they should be requested and authorized (e.g. in writing).

General standards of performance

A statement should be included of the consultant's obligation to exercise reasonable (best, utmost) skill, effort, care and diligence and apply the standards recognized by the international bodies of the profession (a wide variety of terms can be found in various contracts).

Confidentiality

This spells out the consultant's commitment to fully respect confidentiality as defined by the client and not to use any information related to the project and the client organization without prior written authorization of the client. In addition, some clients require each member of the consulting team to sign a similar commitment.

Conflict of interest

Statements are made concerning the avoidance of conflict of interest, such as a prohibition on engaging in conflicting activities and dealings, or on accepting commissions, discounts and similar payments in connection with the assignment.

Behaviour and discipline at work

This covers an obligation to comply with local legislation, and respect work relations and practices formally established or customary in the client environment (if this is in the interest of the assignment).

Consultant's personnel

A description of the profile of personnel acceptable to the client for the performance of the assignment, and of the procedure to be followed by the consultant in submitting personnel to the client's approval, should form part of the contract. The list of the personnel (with curriculum vitae) proposed and accepted by the signature of the contract should be given in an appendix to the contract. Furthermore, the contract would outline the reasons and procedure for replacing consultant personnel at either the consultant's or the client's request. Finally, there should be a reference to the consultant's senior and managerial staff responsible for the backstopping and supervision of the assignment (it should be made clear if time spent by these personnel on the assignment is chargeable to the client).

Subcontracts

Subcontracts proposed by the consultant and approved by the client should be described. The names of the subcontractors will be given if they are known, and the agreed procedure for finding, recruiting and replacing future subcontractors will be outlined.

Reporting

Regular reporting is essential for assignment management and control by both the client and consultant, so the contract should be most precise on the purpose, scope, form and timing of interim and final reports to be submitted by the consultant.

Obligations of the client

Because most consulting projects are collaborative assignments involving intensive consultant-client interaction, it would be unreasonable for the consultant to make a legal commitment if the client is not clear about his inputs and contributions to the assignment. The contract may include a general statement concerning the client's commitment to provide the consultant with information and access to documentation, premises and facilities, to react promptly on all proposals and other matters referred to the client by the consultant, in particular if decisions are needed to carry on with the assignment, and generally to assist the consultant in the discharge of his duties. More specifically, the following points may be covered in this section:

Client's personnel

This gives a description of the functional profiles and number of client personnel assigned to the project, with the indication of the duration and nature of assignment if possible (full-time assignment, assignment for certain activities and limited periods of time, whether these personnel shall take instructions from the consultant or not, etc.). The client's personnel must be acceptable to the consultant. In particular, the client will have to indicate the principal liaison officer for the project.

Support services and facilities

A listing (as complete and precise as possible) should be given of services and facilities such as office space and equipment, secretaries, typists, administrative assistants, translators, interpreters, reproduction and telecommunication facilities, vehicles, drivers, etc. (in particular, it must be clear who is responsible for the typing and reproduction of assignment reports and other documents).

Freedom from taxation and duties

A statement (if applicable) should be made whereby the client warrants that the consultant will be exempt from taxes, duties and other impositions under the applicable law and international agreements, or that the client will pay on behalf of the consultant.

Assistance in obtaining permits

The contract should include a listing of permits, authorizations and clearances (visas, work permits, residence permits, customs clearance, etc.) that will be obtained by the client for the consultant. Alternatively, the client will assist the consultant in obtaining such permits.

Confidentiality

It is often overlooked that it may be appropriate for the client to make a commitment to respect confidentiality in using information obtained from the consultant.

Payments to the consultant

In this section the contract (possibly supplemented by a more detailed appendix) will describe the financial terms of the assignment using the fee and payment formulas chosen (see Chapter 5 for alternative fee and billing practices).

Consultant fees

Details are given of the agreed fee formula and fee rates, e.g. by categories of personnel and sorts of job to which different fees may be applicable. There may be an indication of financial ceilings up to which the fees would be paid.

Reimbursable expenses

Travel, subsistence allowance, communication, document acquisition and reproduction, testing, computing and other authorized expenses will be listed. In international projects of longer duration these expenses may be quite important, and therefore the contracts may also give budget estimates and/or limits for these expenses and stipulate expenses that require the client's prior authorization.

Currency and mode of payment

The contract has to be absolutely clear as regards cost and expense items to be paid in foreign (usually freely convertible) and local (possibly non-convertible or with limited convertibility) currencies. It will indicate the modalities of payment (bank transfer, check, cash, etc.) and the account numbers to be used.

Billing and payment schedule

The billing and payment schedule to be used by the parties (as described in section 5.4) are included, separating the fees from reimbursable expenses. The contract will stipulate the supporting documentation to be submitted with the bills, and indicate if and under what circumstances the client might withhold payment. There will be a precise description of conditions to be fulfilled in order to make final payments (documentation provided, final report, performance checks, quality audit, etc.).

Bonds and guarantees

This consists of a description of performance and other bonds and guarantees to be provided by the consultant (as described in section 5.5) and of the ways in which the bonds can be called.

Price adjustment clauses

International practice recommends price adjustment clauses in contracts of over one year's duration. In a two-year contract, the time-based rates for the second year may already be adjusted to the expected cost-of-living and other price increases. Longer contracts should define a mechanism for reviewing the rates applied on the basis of official data on cost and price indices, and not merely the consultant's decision to charge more. It should also be decided whether the price of a lump-sum contract should be adjustable and under what circumstances.

Record keeping and audits

Most contracts require the consultant to maintain records which clearly identify relevant time and expense. The client is authorized to have these records audited by an accounting firm of his choice, with the exception of agreements where flat (lump-sum) fees are used.

Commencement, completion, alteration and termination of the contract

Effectiveness of contract

A definition should be given of the date on which the contract comes into force and effect. This would normally be the date of the last signature necessary to complete the contracting formalities. In contracts financed by international development banks, an approval by the bank is normally a condition of effectiveness.

Commencement of operations

The operations should start at the dates given in the agreed timetable, or within a fixed time limit (say 30 days) after the effective date.

Expiration of contract

A fixed date for contract expiration may be given, or the text may stipulate that the contract shall terminate when the contracted services have been completed and the payments to the consultant made.

Alterations

Either the consultant or the client should be able to make written proposals for altering the scope and timing of the services owing to changed circumstances and requirements. In addition, the contract should foresee periodic reviews (in periods reflecting the nature of the activity and the duration of the project – say, every six or 12 months) where necessary alterations would be discussed and agreed.

Termination by client

The client must have the right to terminate the contract at any point without giving a reason. There will, however, be a mandatory notice (which could be one week in a simple management advisory assignment, but 30-60 days in a major engineering consultancy). If the client wishes to terminate the contract owing to poor performance of the consultant, a precise procedure should be followed (giving the reasons in writing, asking for reply and immediate action, etc.) and the notice may be shorter.

The contract will also determine the payments to be made on premature termination. The client may agree to pay an indemnity (e.g. 20 per cent of the remaining fees, or fees for one month of work) if he has terminated the contract for a reason other than the consultant's poor performance. Alternatively, there will be no provision for any indemnity.

Termination by consultant

The consultant must be able to withdraw from the contract under certain circumstances, e.g. if he does not get paid although his invoices have not been contested in writing, or if the operations have been suspended for a defined period of time. Here, too, the contract would stipulate the procedure to be observed, including the notice to be given to the client. If the client has been declared bankrupt, the consultant can normally terminate the contract without notice.

Termination or suspension due to force majeure

International contracts include many different definitions of *force majeure*, i.e. circumstances created by events beyond the client's and the consultant's control, such as war, riots, earthquakes, floods and similar, due to which the execution of the contract may become impossible or impractical. Furthermore, the contracts describe the procedure to follow in order to suspend, reactivate or terminate the services.

Liability and insurance

The definition of the consultant's liability, its limits and appropriate insurance is an important part of the contract. The client and the consultant are going to choose applicable (governing) law and the consultant's liability will be determined under that law. Thus, there may be no need for any specific provision in the contract if in the applicable law the definition of liabilities arising from the provision of professional services is precise and detailed enough. However, there are differences in the treatment of liability questions in various legal systems and both the client and the consultant should acquaint themselves with the differences that may concern their contract.

In drafting and negotiating the contract, the consultant may wish to include a provision to limit his liability. This is understandable, provided that this limitation complies with the applicable law. To protect his interest, the client may find it useful to refer to several principles reflecting the experience of the World Bank:

○ A clause stating that the consultant is not liable at all for damages he may have caused in carrying out the contractual services would be unacceptable.

○ A monetary limitation of liability should not apply to damages caused by gross negligence or wilful misconduct.

○ The monetary limitation should be related to the likely damages, but as a practical measure it can be restricted to the amount of the consultant's resources plus his professional insurance. In any case, the limitation should not be less than the contract amount including reimbursables.

○ A consultant should not be indemnified by the client for the damage caused by the consultant to third parties.

Furthermore, the contract should stipulate the insurance that the consultant is required to take. This includes insurance for professional liability (indemnity), third-party liability and any other liability that may be appropriate in the context of the given assignment. The client can require the consultant to provide evidence that he is properly insured. If the client insists on insurance coverage that exceeds what can be regarded as established practice, he may have to reimburse the cost of such insurance, or increase in insurance, to the consultant.

General provisions

This section sets certain general conditions of the contract.

Governing law

The applicable law whereby the contract will be governed is mentioned here. Most consultants will insist, on the advice of their professional associations, in using the law of their home country. Conversely, many clients, especially in the public sector, refuse to use any other than the client's country law. This is a matter to be considered and negotiated early enough in preparing the contract, since the choice of the governing law will affect the drafting of some sections of the contract.

Language

This specifies the language to be used in all matters related to the meaning and interpretation of the contract, and in performing the services stipulated by the contract.

Documents prepared under the contract and copyright

Two diametrically different interpretations of document ownership and copyright are used in drafting consulting contracts:

Contracts originating in consultants' circles, including model contracts and terms of business issued by associations, normally state that "the consultant retains copyright of all documents prepared by him" (FIDIC). The client can of course use the documents for the purpose related to the assignment, but needs the consultant's permission for other uses.

Contracts originating in clients' circles, and in agencies representing clients (e.g. model agreements used in the public sector of various countries), stress that the client should receive the benefits of the work product since he has financed it. According to this conception, all plans, drawings, specifications, designs, reports and other documents prepared by the consultant within the framework of the assignment belong to the client, and copyright rests with the client.

Location

This names the venue where the contract operations shall be executed, and/or states the client's right to designate such venues (which can be in several countries).

Authorized representatives

Names, functions and addresses are given of client's and consultant's representatives authorized to sign the contract and its amendments, invoices and other official documents, and correspondence concerning the execution of the contract.

Resolution of disputes

This section would normally open with a statement on the parties' intention to use their best efforts to avoid conflicts and settle disputes. It will then define a mechanism for formal settlement of disputes arising out of or relating to the contract which cannot be settled amicably.

Current international practice uses arbitration in 99 per cent of cases. The parties agree on the rules of arbitration, which might be the Rules of Conciliation and Arbitration of the International Chamber of Commerce, the UNCITRAL (United Nations Commission on International Trade Law) Arbitration Rules, or many others. Most countries have their national arbitration rules and procedures, such as those of the American Arbitration Association (AAA) in the United States.

The section may end by stating that the resulting awards shall be final and definitive (if permitted by the applicable law) and that the parties shall waive their right to appeal.

---

[1] FIDIC: *The White Book Guide, with other notes and documents for consultancy agreements* (Lausanne, 1991).

[2] World Bank: *Sample form of contract for consultants' services* (Washington, DC, Mar. 1989).

ON WORKING
WITH A CONSULTANT

7

Let us assume that, thanks to careful preparation and successful negotiation, you have been able to sign a contract with the consultant of your choice. The consultant is ready to start and you would like to proceed with the assignment without delay.

At this point you may find it useful to glance through this chapter, which proposes to take you through a number of practical steps and common client concerns involved in starting and operating a consulting assignment.

Throughout the chapter, we shall be looking at two groups of different, yet closely interwoven issues:

o   organizational and procedural issues, such as briefings, work scheduling, definitions of responsibilities, progress monitoring and reporting;

o   interpersonal and behavioural issues, concerning the roles played by the two parties, the factors encouraging or hampering collaboration, resistance to change and factors influencing transfer of expertise and learning.

It is often not realized that even if there is a common desire to draw maximum benefits from the assignment and no intention whatsoever to make difficulties, the consultant is entering the client system as a new element from the outside, and his arrival will disturb the routine course of events. Something will change and this change may have unforeseen effects. Many people will be expected to make a special effort and their workload will increase. Personality clashes may occur despite the best intentions to avoid them. New opportunities will be discovered, which may necessitate a change in the assignment plan.

As a client, you will have to face and resolve all these issues. The consultant is likely to be helpful since he is aware of the problems common to most clients and accepts full responsibility for the behaviour and performance of his own staff. Yet it is the client who is in charge and has the ultimate responsibility for controlling the assignment and taking corrective measures when they are required.

7.1. Organizing for the consultancy

It is frustrating and wasteful if the consultant turns up as agreed and finds the client unprepared. Before the actual start of operations, it is good practice on the client side to check if the organization is ready to receive the consultant and start working according to the schedule provided in the contract. A final check is especially important if some time has elapsed since contract signature.

Assignment of responsibilities

The contact person, or liaison officer, who will provide continuous liaison with the consultant, must be available and fully briefed. As a rule, the liaison officer will be a close collaborator of the "principal" or "primary" client – the manager in the work sector of the consulting assignment. He will have to consider when and how to involve other managers and employees in discussing the work programme and any significant aspects of the assignment. This is a technical function, not an administrative one. The liaison officer will have more opportunity to learn from the consultant than anybody else and this may be beneficial to his future career.

Other people who will have specific tasks in the assignment ought to be designated and briefed about the nature and scope of their involvement. They should know how much time they will have to allocate, what sorts of questions they should discuss with the consultant and what documentation they should provide. Briefing on confidentiality issues is important if the assignment should not touch on certain issues that management has decided to exclude.

Office accommodation and services

The quality of office accommodation will reflect the importance attached to the assignment. Generally speaking, if you pay a high fee to an adviser it is appropriate to provide him with a work environment where he can be fully productive. Consultants do not need luxury office space, but they need more than a small table in a corner or permission to use a meeting room if there is no meeting. They require privacy for interviews and work meetings, and a quiet place for study and drafting. Furthermore, their productivity will be greatly influenced by the availability of secretarial and administrative support, reproduction facilities, computer services, telecommunications, transport between various parts of the client organization, and so forth.

Other facilities and support

In international assignments, the material conditions for an effective start of an assignment may go far beyond office space and arrangements within the client organization. The client may either have a contractual obligation, or will wish to be as helpful as possible, to accommodate the consultant and his family, help with customs clearances and work permits, provide or find a driver and a translator, and so on. Experience shows that even if the client has no formal obligation in these and similar matters, it is useful to help the consultant since this will increase his efficiency and commitment right from the start of the job.

7.2. Introducing and briefing the consultant

In preparing an assignment, the contacts between the client and consultant organizations are normally limited to a few people on each side. This will change with the start of the assignment. The consultant may bring in more people and some of them will come to the client organization for the first time. On the client side the rumours may have spread that a new assignment is about to start and it is quite possible that incomplete information is circulating and people start speculating about the hidden agenda of the consultancy.

Announcing the consultant's arrival

The start of a consultancy ought to be properly announced and the consultant ought to be introduced to people in the client organization. Often it is better to give enough information before the consultant arrives. This may be done in a staff meeting, or by a circular memorandum if many people in various units are to be informed. The consultant's arrival is then an opportunity for introducing him to managers and other staff as appropriate. Since people have been informed beforehand, they will not be caught by surprise.

It is unproductive if the consultant has to introduce himself and explain the purpose of the assignment each time he makes a contact within the client organization. For understandable reasons, many people will resent hearing the first time about the assignment from the consultant and not from their own management. Everything can be gained and nothing lost by informing people properly and soliciting their collaboration at an early stage. Also, people in the organization should learn from their own management, not from the consultant, what information is to be given to him because it is related to the object of the assignment.

To inform the trade unions about the consulting assignment and the presence of consultants in the organization is good management practice in many countries. This may be particularly important if the assignment is likely to touch on issues which are the subject of collective bargaining, or other issues that the trade unions have been negotiating or examining jointly with management.

The consultant's actual arrival in the organization may be a good opportunity for calling a special introductory meeting of people who will be involved, where management would provide an up-to-date overview of the assignment, and the consultant would outline his approach and solicit collaboration and support. He might add recent information on his firm and a little gossip on the consulting industry.

A confidential mangement consulting assignment is another matter. Confidentiality may not permit a wide circulation of complete information. However, many people will learn about the start of the assignment anyway, and a leak of information will encourage speculation and gossip about hidden agendas and real purposes pursued by management. Therefore, it may be better to give at least some information and explain that everything cannot be said before the job is terminated.

Briefing the consultant

Briefing the consultant who comes to your organization is even more important than briefing your people about the consultant. As a client, you have agreed to purchase the consultant's time and you will be paying for it even if it is wasted. A part of this time will certainly be wasted if the consultant has to collect with difficulty and virtually dig out information that is readily available and should be given to him on arrival. Some clients feel that by giving too much information they actually do the job of the consultant who will thus have an easy time and only repackage the information already gathered and analysed by the client. This, however, means that the client has never properly defined the objective of the consultancy and the specific technical contribution that the consultant will have to make over and above the work already undertaken by the client and his staff.

7.3. Working together

A consulting assignment is like a marriage. A new relationship is established and sealed by a legal contract. The partners agree to work together towards a common goal and there are valid reasons for keeping the relationship solid and productive. At the same time there are some centrifugal forces and the partners themselves may behave in a way that will break the contract.

Learning to know each other and speaking frankly about the risks and pitfalls before signing the contract helps, but provides no guarantee that everything will work smoothly and elegantly. The assignment has to be co-managed by the parties with the objective of avoiding misunderstanding and conflicts and strengthening the relationship. The crucial concern of this co-management is the human side of the consultant-client relationship.

Understanding each other

Consultants are trained to be flexible and easily adaptable people and know that in client organizations they will work with different cultures and personalities. But all consultants are not equally sensitive and skilled in interpersonal relations and organizational behaviour. While some are born diplomats and trained psychologists, others are efficient technicians keen to move on with the task at hand, but less sensitive to human problems of organizations.

It is essential to learn about personalities in the consulting team as early as possible. This information cannot be found in the curricula vitae which are conspicuously silent about personality traits, although clients should be informed about them. The consultant's representatives may be able to give you some, but not all, information. More can be found through interviews, informal talks and direct work contacts.

On the other hand, you should help the consultant to understand personalities on your side. Ideally, personalities should be matched. It is not difficult to find out, after a short time of common work, who appreciates and enjoys the other person's attitudes, work methods and behaviour. Some people expect a more directive attitude and a more precise definition of requirements by the consultant, while others prefer a more general invitation to contribute and a more global definition of the tasks, which gives them the opportunity to come up with their ideas and concepts and exhibit initiative. A high degree of tolerance can be expected and even required on both sides, since absolutely perfect matching of personalities is virtually impossible.

The impact of culture

The client's and the consultant's cultures play a major role in assignments. By culture we mean collectively shared values, beliefs, traditions and behavioural norms unique to a particular group of people. People create culture as a mechanism that helps them to cope with their environment and maintain the cohesion and identity of the community in interacting with other communities.

The consultant will need to find out about your organizational or corporate culture, since this will affect his work strategies and methods. For example, he will need to learn about your organization's values and behavioural norms concerning:

o   the mission and image of the organization;

o   centres of influence;

o   the decision-making and consultation processes;

o   management's and employees' support for innovation and change and ability to cope with change;

o   management and leadership styles;

o   circulation and sharing of information;

o   confidentiality and secrecy;

o   ways of handling conflict;

o   management's and employees' identification with the organization.

You may be able to brief your consultant on your organization's culture, in particular if some former studies have diagnosed and described it. Alternatively, the issue may be as new and delicate to you as to the consultant. In such a case, it will be useful to give some thought to your organization's culture. This will be helpful not only for the current assignment, but for dealing with many other strategic and organizational issues in the future.

If the consultant comes from a foreign country, he needs to be briefed on the national culture, or cultures, in which your organization is implanted. While you can suppose that your consultant was briefed on your country, you cannot be sure that this briefing was full and correct. In many cases, the consultant's briefing will be superficial and incomplete, based on journalistic oversimplifications and stereotypes. You will have to rectify this, helping the consultant not to be misled by information presenting your national environment, and the impact of this environment on your organization, differently from the reality.

The complex cultural factors and influences that are present on your side are also present on the consultant's side. The consultant is affected by his culture whether he is aware of it or not. In certain cases his culture may even prevent the consultant from being effective in your organizational environment. Therefore it is in every client's interest not to assume that there cannot be any cultural problems, and to find out as much as possible about the consultant's culture.

If the consultant comes from a well-established consulting firm with some traditions and a certain reputation, you will want to learn enough about the professional culture of that particular firm (elitist attitudes and behaviours, entrepreneurial spirit, absolute honesty or willingness to compromise at ethical issues, fixed fees or readiness to bargain, relationships between the accounting and consulting sectors in the firm, career paths and consultant motivation factors, and similar). The firm's representatives will willingly discuss most of these issues with you and will speak proudly about values and norms thanks to which the firm has gained its professional reputation and image. They will be less open in talking about organizational culture issues that might be perceived as negative (if they are aware of them).

Furthermore, you will wish to consider whether the consultant's national culture can have any impact on working relations with your organization. Many consultants active in foreign countries have become aware of their own cultural strengths and weaknesses through experience and by means of special training workshops dealing with cultural issues. This, however, does not apply to all consultants without exception. Generally speaking, you should encourage your consultant to give thought to his own culture and the differences from yours. Once the basic relationship of trust has been established, many of these issues, including even the more delicate religious, ethnic and political issues, can be discussed amongst the consulting organization's and your firm's staff. If you are aware of cultural differences between you and your consultant, you should take the initiative to discuss these issues with him. Both of you will benefit from such a discussion.

It is of little use to criticize the consultant behind his back for behaviour that is unusual in your environment. The consultant is at the client's service and a tactful way can be found for taking up any issue that may irritate the client.

Managing change

A common purpose of various consulting assignments is to help organizations in planning and implementing change. Every assignment, including the one you may just be dealing with, is somehow related to changes that are being envisaged or are being implemented by your organization. In planning and managing a consulting assignment, it is therefore necessary to be aware of the roles it will play in organizational change, and of some general principles of managing change.

The main difficulty with organizational change is that it is both wanted and resented by people. On the whole, people understand that they cannot live without change, which is an inherent characteristic of both human life and economic and social systems. People are prepared to cope with organizational changes if they see and can endorse their purpose and benefits. Yet it is rare for an organizational change project, even if it is a consultant-assisted project, not to meet with any resistance.

The ILO guide to management consulting[1] points out eight principal reasons for resistance to change in organizations, as summarized in table 7.1. Many of these reasons can be traced to incompetent handling of changes by managers and consultants: people in the client organization are not properly informed, do not understand the purpose and the degree of necessity of the changes, are not consulted on how the changes should be made and generally feel ill-treated.

Table 7.1. Reasons for resistance to change

- **Lack of conviction that change is needed.** If people are not properly informed, and the purpose of change not explained to them, they are likely to view the present situation as satisfactory and an effort to change as useless and upsetting.

- **Dislike of imposed change.** In general, people do not like to be treated as passive objects. They resent changes that are imposed on them and about which they cannot express any views.

- **Dislike of surprises.** People do not want to be kept in the dark about any change that is being prepared; managerial decisions bringing about important changes tend to be resented if they come as a surprise.

- **Fear of the unknown.** Basically, people do not like to live in uncertainty and may prefer an imperfect present to an unknown and uncertain future.

- **Reluctance to deal with unpopular issues.** Managers and other people often try to avoid unpleasant reality and unpopular actions, even if they realise that they will not be able to avoid these for ever.

- **Fear of inadequacy and failure.** Many people worry about their ability to adjust to change, and to maintain and improve their performance in a new work situation. Some of them may feel insecure, and doubt their ability to make a special effort to learn new skills.

- **Disturbed practices, habits and relations.** Following organizational change, well-established and fully mastered practices and work habits may become obsolete, and familiar relationships may be altered or totally destroyed. This can lead to considerable frustration and unhappiness.

- **Lack of respect and trust in the person promoting change.** People are suspicious about change proposed by a manager whom they do not trust and respect, or by an external person whose competence and motives are not known and understood.

The client and the consultant will need to discuss the change strategy and methods to be used in the assignment. This will concern questions such as:

○ whether, at what stage of the process and in what way to involve people in designing and implementing organizational changes in order to enlist support, tap their wisdom and prevent resistance;

○ what change measures will require negotiation, possibly including negotiation with trade unions;

o   what change measures (if any) may have to be imposed if resistance to change cannot be overcome;

o   what pace of change will be feasible and manageable;

o   in what part of the organization should the change process start;

o   whether there should be a pilot or experimental project;

o   how to identify and use "champions" – people who will accept and apply new ideas more easily and more rapidly than others, become their keen promoters and help by demonstrating what can be achieved;

o   what objections to change can be expected from whom, and what will be the best way of handling objections;

o   what information, training and other support should be provided to people to facilitate changes;

o   what will be the client's leadership role throughout the change process, in particular in difficulties and crises;

o   what will be the consultant's function and behaviour.

The client should not try to unload the prime responsibility for planning and managing change from his shoulders and transfer it to the consultant. Yet the consultant can play a major and even critical role if he is versed in organizational change issues and perceived as a competent professional who is genuinely interested in providing help and whom people in the client organization can trust and respect.

The consultant's roles in the change process

The consultant will play a role in the change process and have some impact on people's attitudes to change in any event. It has been observed that the very presence of the consultant, and the fact of asking a few neutrally worded questions about current work methods and problems, bring about some changes. Change will start before any proposals are submitted, discussed and approved. Conversely, the consultant's clumsy behaviour may generate resistance to change before any specific changes are mentioned.

During the assignment, the consultant will be doing various things, and will be seen by people doing these things. Often it will be possible to choose among different consultant behaviours depending on the situation: a behavioural pattern that encourages and supports change in one organizational and cultural context may have adverse effects in another context. Furthermore, the client and the consultant should be prepared to change the roles played as the situation evolves, different tasks are successively tackled, and people's skills and attitudes develop during the assignment.

Thus, if change is hampered by a lack of competence and people feel that working with the new method would be too difficult, the consultant should help by demonstrating the method, training and explaining how to avoid errors. If people resist change, the consultant may be well placed to identify the real causes of this resistance and help the client in convincing people that change is necessary and benefits can be achieved. If people do not appreciate the seriousness of environmental threats, such as new competition due to market deregulation, or unexpected technological change, the consultant can help the client to shake up their self-satisfaction and stop viewing the external world through rose-coloured spectacles.

In these and similar situations, the consultant must be able to help the client to focus on approaches and arguments that motivate people and build their consensus and commitment to change.

Resolving conflict

Aware of their roles of advisers and helpers, most consultants have learned to avoid behaviour which irritates people and creates conflict with the client or some of his staff. Yet they are unable to avoid conflictual situations totally. In consulting, the causes of conflict can be:

o   poor communication;

o   disagreement on objectives and results to be achieved;

o   disagreement on intervention methods;

o   differences over the pace of change;

o   resistance to change;

o   fear of losing influence and power;

o   competition for resources;

o   non-respect of commitments;

o   refusal to cooperate;

o   personality and culture clashes;

o   poor performance and inefficiency.

In certain cases it may be necessary to let the conflict develop and become open so that the real issue can be identified and addressed. Yet it is more effective if the client and the consultant can anticipate conflict and try to address the causes before the conflict becomes open.

HOW TO SELECT AND USE CONSULTANTS: A CLIENT'S GUIDE

As Gordon Lippitt pointed out, it is advisable to depersonalize conflict by ensuring that the disputants do not sit in judgement over each other, and to focus the conflict on the basic issue by concentrating disagreement on factual ground. He suggests the following five principal methods of interpersonal conflict resolution:[2]

○ **withdrawal**: retreating from an actual or potential conflict situation;

○ **smoothing**: emphasizing areas of agreement and de-emphasizing areas of difference over conflictual areas;

○ **compromising**: searching for solutions that bring some degree of satisfaction to the conflicting parties;

○ **forcing**: exerting one's viewpoint at the potential expense of another – often open competition and a win/lose situation;

○ **confrontation**: addressing a disagreement directly and in a problem-solving mode – the affected parties work through their disagreements.

If possible, priority should be given to achieving an agreement by smoothing, compromising and confrontation since they permit the parties to the dispute to address the issue and arrive at a win/win situation. Withdrawal avoids the issue, but the solution may be only temporary. Forcing uses authority and power and can even deepen the conflict, but may be necessary in extreme cases where agreement obviously cannot be achieved amicably.

If there is conflict, it will usually concern the consultant's relations to certain persons in the client organization affected by the assignment. The client and the consultant should consider jointly if they are able to cope with the conflict and how to approach it.

7.4. Learning from the consultant

Learning from consulting is not automatic even if it was defined as a key objective of the assignment. Learning occurs only if it is pursued by both the client and the consultant as a specific operational objective rather than a vaguely defined general principle. The reason is that, in the execution of an assignment, many variables intervene which hamper learning and detract attention from it.

The time factor

Shortage of time, not a lack of interest, is the principal obstacle. Since most consulting assignments create a temporary additional workload, often the client is happy if the consultant proceeds with the job without asking too many questions, requesting detailed documentation and creating a further additional workload for the client's staff. The task is accomplished, but the client does not know how it was done. The opportunity has been missed. As this happens again and again, it is important to assess realistically the time implications of the client's participation when the assignment is being planned, as well as during all monitoring meetings.

The consultant's and the client's attitudes

The consultant can help by gently, though persistently, pressing the client to be available, spend more time with the consultant, assign capable collaborators to him, take care of work for which the consultant's skills are not required, and so on. Some consultants are reluctant to adopt this attitude, the result being that the client participates less and less even if the original plan was to involve him actively.

The consultant must, of course, be willing and have the patience to share expertise, explain and justify the approach taken, show where and how to retrieve information, let the client staff produce first drafts and improve them afterwards, pass on information on the diagnostic and other methodologies used, and so on. The client, on the other hand, must not be reluctant to ask questions and make an effort to become fully involved. The consultant has been recruited in order to provide expertise, so ask specific and detailed questions, and ask again and more of them. Do not worry that your questions might look silly to the consultant. No client has ever lost face by trying to obtain more information and learn more from his consultant.

Structured training events

In addition to informal on-the-job learning during joint work with the consultant on a common task, it is often foreseen to schedule specific training events. The advantage is that distinct inputs related to the main topic of the assignment can be covered in a systematic manner, time is allocated and other people can be invited in addition to the consultant's direct collaborators among the client's staff. Often it is useful to foresee different types of training event for the people who will be directly involved in the new scheme, and for those (e.g. managers, supervisors and staff in other functional areas) who should be kept informed although their involvement will not be direct.

The preferred forms of training include:

o   on-the-job training by doing specific tasks with the consultant or under his supervision; and

o   workshop sessions in which all aspects of the new technique or scheme can be reviewed in depth and detail in an active discussion, not just by listening to a consultant's presentation.

There are many other suitable forms of in-service training which can be arranged by the consultants, such as study visits and attachments to other companies where a similar problem was faced and resolved. These may be foreign companies where the consultant has worked previously, or which he can identify thanks to his connections.

7.5. Reporting during the assignment

Reporting is one of the principal tools used in controlling consulting assignments. With the exception of very short assignments, the assignment plan will foresee several progress or interim reports to be drafted and submitted by the consultant. The consultant may also produce technical reports on specific subjects treated by the assignment. These technical reports may even be the main tangible products of the assignment, e.g. in feasibility or sectoral studies, or in diagnostic surveys of training needs.

Progress reports

The purpose of a progress report is to give a true and complete picture of the work performed and progress made by the assignment. A longer assignment would be divided into several report periods, which may be calendar year periods (e.g. quarterly or six-monthly reports), or periods corresponding to major phases in the consulting process (report at the end of the diagnostic phase, etc.). Progress reports are particularly important in assignments where the consultants work essentially on their own, without intensive client involvement, and the client needs to receive regular information on what is actually happening.

The design of progress reports must facilitate their use in assignment control and monitoring. A good progress report is short, concise, simply structured and clearly worded, drawing management's attention to the main achievements of the period under review and corrective measures required. A progress report is not a piece of literature, but a practically focused paper for managerial action. Its essential elements cover:

o   work performed;

o   resources used;

o   progress made towards interim and final objectives and targets;

o   obstacles encountered;

o   new problems discovered;

o   new ideas and opportunities brought to the client's attention;

o   staffing and other difficulties;

o   suggestions for adjustments in the assignment schedule;

o   suggestions for any other action by the client and the consultant.

Progress reports are to be submitted within a few days (not weeks) of the report period, and acknowledged and reviewed immediately. They can be discussed in assignment review meetings, or merely acknowledged if no discussion is necessary.

If interim evaluation is foreseen, as will be discussed in section 7.6, the main progress reports normally coincide with key interim evaluation exercises and are reviewed at evaluation meetings.

Technical reports

Technical reports are produced as the result of specific technical tasks undertaken as part of the assignment. Their number and structuring is a matter of convenience. For example, in a diagnosis of training needs, the consultant can be asked to prepare one summary report, or several reports, each covering training needs of one category of personnel or one part of the organization. Often it is convenient to break down the task into several technical reports. This permits action to be taken on the report without waiting until a global technical report, covering a broad problem area, can be completed. Furthermore, the methodology used in preparing the first report might be assessed and improvements reflected in the following reports.

Technical reports deal with a wide range of subjects, and they therefore come in many different forms.

Effective reporting

The drafting of reports uses up precious consultants' time for which the client will pay. The client, in turn, is supposed to study the reports carefully and both parties will spend some time in discussing the conclusions and action to take. It cannot be overemphasized that producing unnecessary reports, as well as lengthy, and poorly structured and drafted ones, is a luxury that few clients can afford.

In planning for the assignment, it is essential to devote some time to the discussion of reporting. The number and size of the reports should be kept to a strict minimum, and it should be clearly established why each report is wanted and what use the client organization will make of it. It is the client's prerogative to decide what reports will be required. The consultant should not use any chargeable time for producing reports that are not wanted.

The consultant may have one or more standard report formats and may show them to you. However, if you have standard report formats that your organization has found practical and which you have been used to, do not hesitate to show them to the consultant. The report format should facilitate the study by the client, not discourage the client from working with the report.

7.6. Monitoring the assignment

There are many reasons why in consulting the real course of operations may deviate from the path originally scheduled and agreed. If you want to keep track of what is actually happening, determine why it differs from what should be happening and apply timely corrective measures, you will need a reliable assignment monitoring system. Such a system can be simple, but it must work – and be seen working – both by the consultant and by your staff involved in the assignment. You will be monitoring both your consultant and your own role in the assignment. You will be looking at all aspects of the assignment, including the behavioural issues, work styles, interpersonal relations and other factors that will influence the progress and the results of the project.

The system is built on a certain number of regularly performed checks related to key aspects of the assignment. Information will be drawn from assignment progress reports, feedback received from the consultant, interviews with your staff, bills received and payments to the consultant, feelings in your management team on how the assignment is progressing, and complaints received. Attention would be paid to the influence of external factors which either directly affect your assignment or mean that the orientation or the schedule of the assignment ought to be reconsidered. This information would be collected and evaluated by yourself or a designated member of your management team, and summarized for management meetings.

The monitoring system may include regular assignment review meetings of the client's and the consultant's representatives, or such meetings can be arranged from time to time, when the consultant's partner or another senior professional comes to supervise the assignment, or when you or the consultant feel that there is a special reason to meet.

Observing the assignment schedule

It is fairly easy to verify if the consultant and the client are providing staff and other inputs in accordance with the agreed schedule. To control work progress and outputs is a more delicate matter, especially in longer and complex assignments if the partial outputs do not easily lend themselves to measurement and assessment. Yet this is where the thrust of monitoring is, despite the difficulties involved. If measurement is impossible or impractical, the staff involved can be asked to estimate the progress made and the likelihood of meeting the deadlines.

Maintaining the assignment focus

In complex consulting assignments, numerous forces and challenges tend to detract the consultant and the client from the original purpose of the assignment, suggesting possible modifications or putting new issues on the table. As a rule, the tendency is to widen the focus, not to narrow it. Valid reasons may be submitted, such as the desirability of examining a greater number of alternatives, increasing precision and depth of diagnostic work or increasing the size of the project to obtain greater benefits. However delicate, the choice has to be made. The client must not let the project widen in an uncontrolled manner whatever the reasons given and the motivation of the people involved.

Assuring quality

The quality of consulting can be greatly improved by monitoring. Right from the beginning of the assignment, both the client and the consultant can compare the quality of the inputs and the tasks performed with the agreed standards, and with standards normally applied in the consulting and the client organizations. This concerns all aspects of the job: the depth and thoroughness of fact finding, the choice of methods for assessing organizational and individual performance, or the consultant's approach to choosing among commercial and customized software for operations scheduling and control. It is important to discuss quality standards during assignment review meetings.

Work style and climate

We have been stressing repeatedly that the consultant can not only play various roles in helping the client organization to implement change, but that these roles can change during the assignment. This is a key topic for assignment monitoring. Throughout the assignment, the dynamics of the consultant's and the client's respective roles need to be regularly reviewed and discussed, to be sure that the roles fit the situation, facilitate change and enable the transfer of expertise to the client. The signals to watch include:

- o   critical comments on the consultant's work style by the client personnel;

- o   the consultant's complaints about a lack of interest or support, and resistance, on the client's side;

- o   personality clashes, tensions and communication blockages;

- o   doubts about the actual chance of the assignment to make any difference;

- o   conflict and disagreement about any aspect of the relationship.

The assignment may be a difficult task and a major challenge requiring many extra hours from everybody. There may be signs of fatigue, impatience and loss of perspective. An opportunity to encourage people, thank them for special efforts and show how important the assignment is to the organization should not be missed during assignment monitoring.

Controlling costs and budgets

The monitoring of financial aspects of the assignment helps to avoid cost overruns, as well as undesirable divergencies from approved budgets and projected cash flows. The following points will be checked:

- o   unforeseen expenses and losses on both the consultant's and the client's side, and higher than budgeted reimbursable expenses;

- o   the cost and cash-flow implications of changes in work schedules and suggested additional work;

- o   the justification of cost increases;

- o   the use of all possibilities to make savings without affecting quality (in particular by eliminating unnecessary work and transferring tasks from the consultant to the client);

- o   the strict observance of billing and payment schedules (clients who are late in paying the bills cause difficulties not only to the consultant but also to themselves, since they may have to make various concessions affecting the work programme);

- o   the disbursement of funds approved for the assignment.

Interim evaluation

The assignment plan and contract may foresee one or more interim evaluation exercises at key intervals in the execution of the assignment. Such an evaluation may be mandatory if the assignment is funded by a loan from a development bank or a technical assistance grant, or the client may decide that the duration and complexity of the assignment justify formal interim evaluation.

Interim evaluation exercises can be regarded as a special form of assignment monitoring. In principle, the evaluators will be looking into the same aspects of assignment progress towards the final objective, and the main purpose will be to take timely corrective measures. Systematic detailed monitoring will, in turn, prepare enough material for interim evaluation reports and meetings.

A mandatory evaluation procedure may stipulate the reports to be submitted, the composition of the evaluation meetings and the treatment to be given to the conclusions from these meetings. The continuation of the project and further disbursement authorization may be contingent upon the results of interim evaluation. Another task of interim evaluation is to prepare final evaluation (see Chapter 8), especially on those aspects of the assignment, such as the consultant's performance, on which information has to be collected and evaluated throughout the assignment.

---

[1] Milan Kubr (ed.): *Management consulting: A guide to the profession* (Geneva, ILO, second (revised) ed., 1986); p. 58.

[2] Gordon Lippitt: *Organizational renewal* (Englewood Cliffs, New Jersey, Prentice-Hall, 1982), p. 151.

ON WINDING UP A CONSULTING ASSIGNMENT

8

With this chapter we are coming to an end of the normal consulting cycle. The consultant's job is nearly completed, or the client believes that he has learned enough from the consultant and can finish the assignment by himself. Both the client and the consultant wish to terminate the assignment amicably and in a professional manner. What remains to be done?

Once more, the difference between assignments and the need to judge each situation on its own merits cannot be overemphasized. Yet there are some common practices that have proved useful in winding up consulting projects. These will be reviewed on the following pages.

8.1. When to terminate the assignment?

The simple answer is when the consultant has completed the job, the results described in the assignment proposal and contract have been attained, and the consultant's presence is no longer necessary. This, however, may be difficult to determine. The client's and the consultant's views may differ, and even within the client organization there may be disagreement on the appropriate timing of assignment termination.

This is due to many factors that are inherent in management and business consulting. There are distinct technical projects where all or most of the work is done by the consultant's team and defining a moment when the project is finished, and can be fully taken over by the client, does not present a problem. However, most consulting assignments are inputs in the complex process of managing the firm and improving organizational performance. Activities and relationships influenced by the assignment will continue after its completion, the difference being that the consultant will no longer be present and the client will have to cope by himself. This is particularly true if process consulting is used, where the consultant does not handle distinct technical tasks on behalf of the client but helps the client to become aware of processes whereby the organization identifies and resolves its problems, and to make these processes more effective. Who can determine, and on what basis, that lasting improvements have been made and the consultant should withdraw?

The question of timely withdrawal ought to be discussed at the beginning of the assignment, together with the results to be achieved and the criteria whereby the assignment will be evaluated. During the assignment, the review meetings provide another opportunity to talk about termination. Termination is not a delicate issue: the consultant knows perfectly well that the assignment will come to an end, and is likely to be preparing for work with other clients.

The most appropriate time for withdrawal is when the client is able to continue the work without the consultant. This can be sooner than originally scheduled in the assignment plan, and if such a conclusion is reached, the consultant should be the one who takes the initiative and offers to withdraw. Staying longer than necessary is unprofessional if the contract is time based. If a flat-fee formula is applied, the client will not pay more if the consultant stays longer. Here the problem may be reversed: preventing the consultant's departure before the job is really completed.

8.2. Evaluating the assignment

The termination of a consulting assignment provides a golden opportunity for thorough evaluation. Without evaluation, it would be impossible to assess the results and draw any lessons for future assignments. Clients who underestimate evaluation and regard it as a waste of resources tend to repeat the same mistakes in choosing and using consultants and can spend a lot of money without being sure of the benefits.

True enough, evaluation is not easy and may even be painful. If it was not foreseen when the assignment was designed and negotiated, both the consultant and the client may be desperately looking for meaningful criteria and convincing figures when the final report is due. In some assignments, it will be difficult to find reliable figures for evaluation if the results are mainly qualitative (e.g. increased competence or improved interpersonal relations) or if quantitative results can be expected at a later stage only. Discouraged by these difficulties, some clients regard evaluation as a superfluous academic exercise, since it has to be based on assumptions and estimates rather than on hard data.

It is the client's prerogative to choose evaluation criteria and take the lead in evaluating any assignment done for him by a supplier of professional services. However, the consultant is also interested in evaluation and will in any case evaluate the assignment for his own benefit. He probably has more experience with evaluation than the client. Therefore it is useful to carry out evaluation jointly in the same spirit of understanding and collaboration which characterized the whole assignment. This does not mean that the client will have to endorse all conclusions suggested by the consultant.

Evaluation of results

If the desired results, or benefits, were defined and agreed on in the assignment proposal and contract, they serve as a basis for comparison with the results identified at the end of the assignment. In addition, there may be unexpected results. Whenever possible, quantifiable and measurable results should be identified and assessed. However, qualitative results and opinions cannot be dismissed, since they may express significant and lasting outcomes of the assignment. The results to be assessed include new performance, new behaviours, new systems and new competencies.

New performance

Superior performance is the bottom line for assessing the results of consulting in management and business. Along with improved economic and financial performance there may also be changes in social indicators, improvements in the impact on the environment, and so on. Improved performance can be measured globally (profits, output, return on investment, etc.) or by more detailed analytical data concerning the sector or activity area where the consultancy was carried out (energy savings in one workshop, reduced labour turnover and absenteeism).

New behaviours

By new behaviours we mean doing things in a different way. A wide range of new behaviours can be the result of a consulting assignment. For example, production management starts holding regular meetings with sales management to review the short-term sales forecasts, the general manager's behaviour is less directive, or the workers actually start using accident-prevention equipment.

New systems

Many assignments aim to modernize management information, scheduling, record keeping, reporting, quality management and other organizational systems. Often the introduction of a new system is a condition of new behaviour, or the system can be brought to a standstill if behaviour does not change. As a rule, it is easy to identify if a new system has been designed and delivered by the consultant. However, it may be more difficult to ascertain if the system is fully operational and will remain so after the consultant's departure. There may be a tendency to continue the old system in parallel with the new one.

New competencies

New competencies include the results of training provided by the consultant to client staff, as well as any other new expertise (knowledge, skill, experience) acquired by the client in working with the consultant on various tasks during the assignment.

When to assess the results

In many assignments it will be impossible to identify and measure all results when the consultants have completed the job and are ready to leave the client organization. The performance and reliability of a new system cannot be established until the system has been in operation for several months or even years. Measures to improve quality may have produced spectacular immediate improvements, but will quality remain high in the medium term?

If project performance cannot be achieved or stabilized – and results measured – until some time later, there is a case for follow-up evaluation to be carried out several months or even a year or two after the end of the assignment. It will be necessary to decide how this decision will influence the final payments of the consultant's fee if it is contingent on results.

Evaluation of assignment design and management

Most interesting and useful lessons can be drawn from the evaluation of the assignment design and the ways in which the consulting process was conducted and managed by the two parties. The purpose is to establish if the design and intervention methods used were suitable for the technical and cultural setting of the client organization and for the particular object of the assignment. The main questions are:

o   Were the scope, focus, objectives and results of the assignment adequate to our needs and clearly defined?

o   Were the duration, timing, scheduling, and organization of the assignment correct?

o   Did we have a well-drafted contract as a basic document for managing the assignment?

o   Were our people properly consulted and briefed?

o   Was the consultant's intervention methodology clearly determined and did it suit our organization? Was it effective?

o   Was the agreed schedule of interim reports and control meetings observed? Did we promptly take corrective measures and make other required modifications?

o   Was the fee formula suitable to the nature of the task?

o   Was the billing and payment schedule respected?

Evaluation of the consultant

In evaluating the consultant, the main purpose is to determine if and under what conditions it would be appropriate to turn again to the same consulting firm and use the same consulting staff. However, the lessons learned will be useful for dealing with other consultants. The following questions should be addressed:

o   Did the consulting firm exhibit full competence and state-of-the-art know-how in the subject area of the assignment?

o   How imaginative, innovative and flexible was the consultant in designing and conducting the assignment?

o   How competent was the operating team assigned to our project? Did they adapt easily to our organization? What was the relationship with our staff?

o   Did the consulting firm's management pay enough attention to our concerns, the conduct of our assignment and the problems faced by the operating team during the assignment?

o   Did the consulting firm take any special initiative and make any unforeseen contribution in connection with the assignment?

o   Did the consultant make enough effort to transfer know-how and expertise to our people?

o   Did the consultant operate efficiently and economically?

o   Does the consultant possess expertise that could be useful to us in the future?

o   Can we recommend the consultant to other clients? Shall we agree to provide referrals at their request?

David Maister has provided a list of questions for evaluating the consultant's work (see table 8.1). The rating can be made by the client at the consultant's request for the benefit of the consultant and the management of his firm. Alternatively, the client may take the initiative in rating the consultant. More and more consulting firms show interest in receiving such open and complete feedback from their clients.

The client's self-evaluation

Because the consultant's and the client's roles in an assignment are communicating vessels, the consultant's evaluation cannot be complete and fair without assessing the client's role. You will probably ask the consultant for a frank assessment of your attitudes and inputs. However, the consultant may be loath to criticize the behaviour of certain people in your organization or

Table 8.1. Questions on which professional firms need their clients' feedback

For each of the following statements about our firm please indicate whether you
- strongly disagree (1)
- somewhat disagree (2)
- neither agree nor disagree (3)
- somewhat agree (4)
- strongly agree (5)

- You are thorough in your approach to your work
- You show creativity in your proposed solutions
- You are helpful in redefining our view of our situation
- You are helpful in diagnosing the causes of our problem areas
- You staff my work well: there is enough senior time
- You staff my work well: you don't have high-priced people doing junior tasks
- You return phone calls promptly
- Your people are accessible
- Your people are courteous
- Your people are helpful when I call
- You keep your promises on deadlines
- You document your work activities well
- You don't waste our time
- Your communications are free of jargon
- You offer fast turnaround when requested
- You listen well to what we have to say
- You relate well to our people
- You keep me sufficiently informed on progress
- You let us know in advance what you're going to do
- You notify us promptly of changes in scope, and seek our approval
- You give good explanations of what you've done and why
- You don't wait for me to initiate everything: you anticipate
- You don't jump to conclusions too quickly
- You involve us at major points in the engagement
- You have a good understanding of our business
- You make it your business to understand our company
- You are up to date on what's going on in our world
- You make us feel as if we're important to you
- You are an easy firm to do business with
- You deal with problems in our relationship openly and quickly
- You keep us informed on technical issues affecting our business
- You show an interest in us beyond the specifics of your tasks
- You have been helpful to me beyond the specifics of your projects
- You have made our people more effective at what they do
- My own understanding of your area has improved from working with you

Thank you for your assistance. Please feel free to add any additional comments.

Source: List used by David Maister and reproduced with his kind permission.

the technical quality of your inputs. Therefore, the feedback received from the consultant should be supplemented by self-evaluation, which is an internal and confidential matter of the client organization. Replies to the following questions can be particularly useful:

o Did we proceed correctly in selecting the consultant?

o Was our participation active enough and commensurate with the importance of the project?

o Did we assign people of the right calibre to work with the consultant?

o Did we use every opportunity for learning from the consultant?

o Did we provide effective feedback to the consultant on his behaviour, pace of work, performance, desired changes in work methods, etc.?

o Was any consultant time and effort wasted due to inefficiency on our side?

o Was the consultant obliged to do work that should have been carried out by our people?

8.3. Final reporting

The notion of consulting reports is closely connected with assignment termination. To many clients, the consultant's final report is the end and the principal product of any consultancy. Once they get a report with recommendations, they regard the consultant's job as completed.

Submitting a final report at some point close to the end of an assignment is normal consultant practice. Final reports are required by nearly all consulting contracts and consultants tend to be well versed in reporting. Unfortunately, many reports are produced just because this has been the routine and the parties could not imagine any other way of closing the assignment. In other cases, consultants use the final report to communicate to the client many important facts and suggestions that could not be communicated during the assignment because the client was too busy or did not assign staff of a proper level to work with the consultant. The report is loaded with excellent information and ideas, but these come a little too late.

What reports are required?

The point is that many clients and consultants either do not attach enough importance to final reports, or fail to define clearly the report's function in the light of the objectives and the structuring of the whole assignment.

It may be useful to stress the difference between a final assignment report and the technical reports that were described in the previous chapter. This difference should be kept in mind even if a technical report is due at the end of an assignment and a decision is taken to merge it with the final assignment report into one comprehensive document.

The purpose of the final report is a critical overview of what was done and achieved during the assignment. Therefore the report describes the work performed and the results obtained, comparing them with the assignment description which was part of the contract. The consultant comments on the differences and explains the reasons such as:

o changes in the business climate and other external factors;

o changes in the client's priorities and business objectives;

o consultant's and client's performance factors that influenced the course and outcome of the assignment.

The assumption is, of course, that the results can be measured and assessed when the report is prepared. If not, there should be a suggestion on how to evaluate the results when the new scheme or technique becomes stabilized, as discussed above.

Risks, weak points, negative developments and unfinished tasks should be mentioned and commented on as well. Some consultants may not be keen to elaborate on these questions if they are not sure how such comments will be received by the client. However, frank comments on what could not be achieved, and on existing and potential problems and risks, could be of greater value to the client than any description of the work performed.

Internal client report

Many organizations that work regularly with consultants have found it useful to produce an internal report on every completed assignment. This report is short, follows a standard outline and is confidential. It does not repeat the consultant's final report, but in a few sentences summarizes the content of the assignment, the results achieved and the assessment made by the consultant and the client. Particular attention is paid to the consultant's performance and conditions of his employment. The report ends with recommendations concerning the further use of the consulting firm and the client's practices concerning the use of consultants. Confidentiality is essential. In particular, the report would not be available to any external consultants. It will be kept in the client's records and files, as discussed in Chapter 3.

8.4. Closing steps and measures

In addition to final evaluation and reporting, the contractual relationship between the consultant and the client involves some other activities and measures at the end of an assignment. This is the time to look again at the terms of the contract and check whether mutual commitments have been properly settled:

o   Has the consultant transmitted all technical reports and documentation in the agreed form and number of copies?

o   Have the reports been reviewed, evaluations made and closing meetings held?

o   Did the consultant ask for permission to mention the assignment in his firm's referrals and was the permission given? Are there any restrictions due to confidentiality?

o   Has the consultant returned all borrowed equipment, documentation, etc.?

o   Have all payments been settled (including reimbursable expenses)? When and on what conditions will the final payments to the consultant be made?

Usually a final review meeting is held at the end of the assignment, where key conclusions from the evaluation are discussed and the settlement of other matters agreed. In winding up important assignments, both the client and the consulting firm would be represented in this meeting by their managing directors or other high-level executives.

8.5. Towards a long-term relationship

To terminate an assignment does not mean that the relationship between the client and the consultant ought to be discontinued. On the contrary, if the assignment produced good results and there is satisfaction on both sides, it would be ineffective to terminate such a relationship due to the completion of a current assignment.

The client's interest

Some clients feel that by maintaining contacts with their consultant after the termination of a major assignment they actually risk becoming dependent on one consultant and signalling to him that he will be getting further work. They fear that such a relationship could prevent them from diversifying the sources of professional expertise and looking for other interesting opportunities.

The clients should think of their firm's long-term interest and decide how to manage the relationship with their consultants. If the consultant has done an excellent job, why break this relationship? Life goes on; the business world and management technologies will be changing and the pace of this change is likely to be swift. Although in the short run you may see no opportunity for another assignment from the same consultant, maintaining the relationship has several advantages:

o   reduced risk and simplified selection for future assignments;

o   availability of quick help for short assignments, follow-up visits and ad hoc consultations;

o   access to technical and business information generated and distributed by many important consulting firms to their long-term clients;

o   possibly a lower cost of future assignments since the consulting firm is familiar with your organization.

Thus, at the end of a successful assignment, the client and the consultant may agree informally that they would keep in touch and that the consultant's name would again be on the short-list for possible future assignments. Otherwise, a formal agreement may be reached on follow-up work to maintain the new scheme in operation and keep improving it, using new knowledge and experience that will be acquired by the consultant.

The consultant's interest

Turning to the consultant, he will of course be interested in maintaining the relationship if you were satisfied by his performance. As we know, professional firms in management consulting and other sectors need repeat business and must make every effort to keep good clients. This is not only a business objective but a strong professional need. Managers of professional firms complain bitterly about clients who, without any apparent reason, severed the links at the end of an assignment although it was completed to the client's entire satisfaction.

ON BECOMING
A COMPETENT USER
OF CONSULTING SERVICES

9

In the preface to this book, we have stressed that consulting can produce good results if consultants are competent at serving clients and clients in using consultants. It is useful to stress this once more in the conclusion, for quite a few managers have used consultants repeatedly, and have spent a lot of money on paying their bills, without ever drawing proper benefit from a consultant's presence in the organization.

Skill and expertise in using consultants come with practice, but practical experience helps only those who evaluate it and draw lessons from it, and seek further and more challenging experience to learn even more. In the previous chapters, we have therefore focused on those practices of selecting and using consultants that seem to produce good results, because they have been applied by scores of clients who take the use of consultants seriously and want to maximize the value they are getting for their money. You may like to try out this experience to see if it also works for you, and then to try it again, to arrive at approaches that suit your organization, your culture and your personality.

In this final chapter we do not propose to repeat and summarize everything that has been said in the previous text. Rather than that, we have chosen a few points that are particularly important to clients who are keen to quickly become more competent users of consulting and other professional services.

9.1. Understanding what consulting is about

First of all, it is preferable neither to have illusions about consulting nor to underrate its potential. Of course consultants are not magic healers who can always be called upon in case of trouble, with a 100 per cent guarantee of recovery. Neither are they (at least most of them) men and women who went into consulting because they failed in management. If this were so, why would the world's best and most astute business corporations spend money on consulting, and turn to consultants again and again?

It is useful to have a balanced and realistic view of consulting. Direct experience with using consultants is essential, but it does not suffice. No manager will ever be able to use and test directly the whole panoply of consulting methods and approaches, and to tap the wide range of knowledge and know-how available from the consulting profession. Therefore information and experience gained indirectly through publications, through managers' and consultants' meetings, business colleagues and friends, social contacts, and other ways, are equally interesting. If you want to be a well-informed user, keep your ears and eyes open, and aim to follow up and obtain information that may be of practical use to your company. We have, of course, in mind information not only on the services available, but on the chemistry of the consulting process: how consultants identify and diagnose problems in organizations, how they work with clients in planning and implementing change and how clients make sure that assignments produce more than nicely bound reports.

9.2. Choosing the best consultant

Thanks to a realistic and balanced view of consulting you will be able to choose your consultant rather than waiting until some consultant chooses you as his target. You will have your criteria and your procedures, and thanks to them you will be able to say that you have done your best to obtain the best expert available. If your company's future is at stake, look for top experts, but remember that you do not need a brain surgeon if you have a cold. The same applies to consultants, lawyers and other professionals.

In choosing your consultant, you will aim to recruit a competent and reliable professional firm of solid reputation. However, in consulting the human relationship is equally if not more important than technical knowledge and know-how. Therefore you will pay great attention to the matching of personalities. The consulting firm of your choice must provide you with individuals who understand you and care for you, whom you trust and with whom you like to work.

Easy entry, liberal markets and rapidly expanding opportunities have also brought black sheep into consulting. Be careful not to recruit imposters and wheeler-dealers in lieu of serious professionals. There are organizations and ways of checking out and testing the consultants that can help to avoid such errors.

9.3. Being your consultant's active partner

Perhaps the main lessons from successful consulting projects concern the client's role. We have mentioned several times in this book and want to stress once more that the client's active participation in the work of the consultant is the main principle of modern consulting. As a client, you are in charge, you will be paying the bill and the assignment is yours and is not the consultant's project. Therefore, it is up to you, not the consultant, to decide to what extent and in what way you will participate in the project. It is, of course, a matter to be discussed and considered jointly with your consultant. For example, you have to be realistic in allocating time to the assignment. If you are a general manager, it would probably be unrealistic to promise your full-time and personal participation over a period of several weeks. However, recruiting an expensive consultant, who may be the best expert in his field, and then letting him work alone, and allowing yourself to feel happy that he does not waste your time, is a short-sighted and self-defeating approach.

Those who understand consulting and problem-solving are familiar with the concept of "problem ownership". If you are the principal owner of the problem, you will be the main person working with the consultant even if this implies a special effort and swallowing a few bitter pills. If the problem ownership is in the hands of other managers and employees in your company, make sure that the problem owners understand why the consultant was brought in, and play the key roles in the assignment.

In summary, reasons for active participation in consulting assignments are numerous:

o   to be in charge and provide leadership;

o   to involve and motivate the problem owners and make them responsible for the results;

o   to tap all expertise that exists within your company;

o   to identify and remove barriers to change;

o   to learn from the consultant;

o   to make sure that the assignment does not get off track and does not waste your resources.

9.4. Pursuing clear objectives

It is useful to regard every consulting assignment as a technical project that serves a specific purpose. If at all possible, problem identification using the organization's own internal resources should precede the decision to call in a consultant. Assignment requests based on vague problem descriptions and superficial thinking should be returned to their authors, with advice to be more thorough and more specific in trying to justify the need for external help. It is quite often the case that such an internal diagnostic exercise, especially if based on group work and looking at the problem from various angles, can go a long way towards analysing and solving the problem, possibly without any consultancy.

However, consultants also play important roles in problem identification. You may feel pretty sure that you have done your homework and that your problem has been clearly identified and described in the terms of reference. Yet experience has taught consultants to review and verify the client's definition of the problem before making any commitments. In many cases, once the consultant is brought in and starts talking to the client, he quickly finds out that the problem originally described as poor marketing is due to an obsolete product line, and similar.

There are, then, cases where the company is clearly in difficulties but, for some reason, no one is able to point out the real problem. The reason may be technical: a lack of managerial and staff competence, or just lack of information needed to assess the problem and its dimensions objectively. Alternatively, the reasons may be human and cultural, resulting from sclerotic management under which the real problem cannot be identified and brought to the surface, since there is too much conservatism, vested interest and company myopia. In these cases the consultant can be brought in at a very early stage, either to be the person who diagnoses the problem in a similar way to a doctor, or to act as a catalyst, helping the client and his people to reveal and recognize the painful truth about mismanagement and an uncertain future.

Whatever the initial context, client-consultant collaboration in the first phases of an assignment should produce a definition of the purpose of the assignment that is as complete and as clear as possible. This may be an iterative process, a gradual approximation. However, good experience suggests that at some point in this process specific objectives will need to be defined and endorsed by both the client and the consultant. Subsequent assignment monitoring and control will refer to these objectives. Moreover, they will be the basis of a final assignment evaluation.

9.5. Learning from every assignment

Properly prepared and designed consulting assignments offer extraordinary learning opportunities. Not only can managers and staff learn the consultant's substantive, diagnostic and change-management skills, but interaction with other colleagues and the teamwork related to the assignment create learning situations that are not available in routine everyday operations. Therefore all modern concepts of consulting emphasize its learning dimension, pointing out that learning does not occur automatically and without any effort. Learning situations are to be created, opportunities sought, time provided, work organization adjusted, and learning objectives set and controlled together with other operational objectives pursued in assignments.

Learning from consulting assignments is facilitated and encouraged by client self-evaluation. It may require a lot of courage, especially if the problem owner, the principal client, has to admit that his involvement was inadequate, assignment monitoring poor and the results uncertain. Yet without assignment evaluation it is unlikely that a client can become more competent in using consultants. It is difficult to decide whether you should use the same consultant again and what should be improved in your approach to planning, negotiating, executing and monitoring assignments. Excellent consulting firms solicit their clients' feedback and evaluation. If asked, they will also provide you with frank and useful feedback, one that is difficult to request and obtain from people who report to you and even from your peers.

9.6. Aiming at the highest professional standards

Professional standards are the principal building-block and unifying agent in the architecture of free and independent professions. Strict adherence to these standards resolves and prevents many problems involved in consultant selection and use. Therefore, to competent clients professional integrity is the fundamental condition of eligibility of any consultant. This requires good knowledge of what the standards of conduct and ethics mean in various professions, and how they are defined and interpreted in various countries. Also, clients should be familiar with the current problems faced by some professional service firms, since these problems have affected professional and quality standards owing to extremely fast growth of the firms, high staff turnover, numerous mergers and acquisitions, tough competition and an aggressive pursuit of higher earnings per partner.

It is fair to say that both business and government clients obtain the consultants and other advisers that they deserve, for professionals do not live and operate in a vacuum, but in closest symbiosis with their private and public sector clients. Therefore the client's role in achieving and maintaining the highest standards of professional services cannot be overemphasized. If you want highly professional, reliable and trustworthy suppliers of professional services, make sure that you help them in their efforts to maintain high standards of professional conduct and ethics.

9.7. Cultivating and diversifying your sources of expertise

In using the services of consultants and other professionals, the first contact is often difficult and if a formal selection procedure is used, a lot of time and money is spent on choosing the consultant. Turning to the consultant, he has also spent a considerable amount of effort on getting a new client, perhaps too much effort to make his first assignment with the new client fully profitable.

If the selection proves to be right and the assignment successful, there is normally a mutual desire to pursue the relationship. The client and the consultant know each other both as organizations and as human beings. Next time the initial contacts and negotiations can be simpler, if they cannot be skipped completely. Furthermore, the consultant will continue to think of his former client's needs and interests and may help him with new information, contacts and ideas. This justifies a solid long-term relationship, which can take the form of repeat business, retainer arrangements, training courses and seminars, occasional meetings, special consultations and so on. The leading consulting firms of all profiles and sizes attach more and more value to their relationships with existing clients and make more and more efforts to deserve these clients' continued confidence.

Nevertheless, total reliance on one consulting firm is regarded as a risky strategy. Other consultants may be able to provide alternative insights in your business, different intervention methods and new management techniques. Tasks and talents should be matched, and if you are looking for a particular type of expertise, there is no reason for confining your choice to consulting firms already known to you.

Furthermore, many clients face an important strategic choice if they need an array of professional services such as various sorts of management consulting expertise, market research, tax advice, engineering expertise, legal services, financial advice, services of investment bankers and brokers, and so on. The choice will be between one firm providing a wider range of professional services, or several independent firms, each providing a specialist service. One view is that every professional firm usually has one area of strength, its core expertise, while other areas have been added to the portfolio for commercial reasons. An opposite view is that by providing a service package professional firms have gone a long way in meeting their clients' needs and improving the coordination of services to their clientèle. The choice is not easy, but has to be made. Here again, the users of services will be guided by their own experience and preferences, as well as by wider experience of the business circles in using the professional service infrastructure.

In larger organizations, there is often scope for expanding and strengthening internal consulting capabilities. Internal consultants can also be used in combined assignments jointly with external consultants, and in preparing and controlling the work of external advisers.

9.8. Defining your organizational policy for choosing and using consultants

A policy is a set of rules governing a certain type of activity. Talking about policies makes sense if these activities are repeated and if, by establishing a policy framework and defining individual policies formally or informally, decision-makers are guided and helped to make the best choices, consistent with the organization's mission and business strategy. For example, a policy concerning the choice of consultants might stipulate that at least three alternative proposals must be obtained and evaluated each time a consultant is to be chosen and a contract signed with him.

In concluding this chapter, and indeed the whole book, we are not going to suggest specific policies suitable for all the different users of professional services. This would be a strange conclusion of a guide that stresses diversity, choice, adaptation to each client's specific conditions (including conditions such as personalities and individual preferences) and innovation. No one can provide standard policy guidelines that would suit the whole public of users of professional services.

Our message will be limited to the desirability to define such policy and base it on good experience. Therefore your policy is likely to be developed in steps, as your experience with professional services becomes richer and more diversified. Also, your policies may change with new experience. However, having a policy, and keeping it flexible and up to date, can be of great help in your organization's efforts to use consultants more effectively. It will increase consistency in defining and applying those approaches that have given you most satisfaction, make sure that experience is shared among all members of your organization who have to make decisions about the use of professional services, and build up your institutional memory.

APPENDICES

USEFUL ADDRESSES

1. National associations of consultants

AUSTRALIA

Institute of Management Consultants in Australia (IMCA)
PO Box 105
Burnside
South Australia 5066

AUSTRIA

*Fachverband Unternehmens-
beratung und Datenverarbeitung*
Wiedner Haupstrasse 63
1045 Vienna

*Vereinigung Oesterreichischer
Betriebs- und Organisations-
berater (VOB)*
Strauchgasse 3
1010 Vienna

BANGLADESH

*Bangladesh Association of
Management Consultants*
98 Malibagh (DIT Road)
Dhaka 1219

BELGIUM

*Association belge des conseils
en organisation et gestion
(ASCOBEL)*
Avenue des Arts, Boîte 4
1040 Brussels

BRAZIL

*Associação Brasileira de Consul-
tores de Organização (ABCO)*
Rua da Lapa 180, COB
20021 Rio de Janeiro

*Instituto Brasileiro dos Consul-
tores de Organização (IBCO)*
Av. Paulista, 326, 7° andar - cj. 77
CEP 01310 São Paulo

BULGARIA

*Bulgarian Association of Manage-
ment Consulting Firms (BAMC)*
6 D Blagoev Boulevard
Sofia 1000

CANADA

*Canadian Association of Manage-
ment Consultants (CAMC)*
Suite 805
121 Bloor Street East
Toronto, Ontario M4W 3M5

*Institute of Certified Management
Consultants of Canada*
Suite 805
121 Bloor Street East
Toronto, Ontario M4W 3M5

CHINA

*China Enterprise Management
Association (CEMA)*
San Li He
Beijing

*Consulting Association of
Shanghai (CAS)*
c/o 81 Wu Xin Road
Shanghai

CROATIA

*Croatian Management
Consulting Association*
Krsnjavoga 1
41000 Zagreb

CZECH REPUBLIC

Czech Association for
Consulting to Business (ACB)
Slezská 7
12056 Prague 2

DENMARK

Den Danske Sammenslutning af
Konsulenter I Virksomhedsledelse
(DSKV)
c/o Schobel & Marholt/AIM
Dyregardsvej 2
2740 Skovlunde

Foreningen af Management-
konsulenter (FMK)
Kristianagade 7
2100 Copenhagen OE

FINLAND

Liikkeenjohdon Konsultit (LJK)
Pohjantie 12A
02100 Espoo 10

FRANCE

Chambre syndicale des sociétés
d'études et de conseils (SYNTEC)
3 rue Léon Bonnat
75016 Paris

Office professionel de
qualification des conseils
en management
3 rue Léon Bonnat
75016 Paris

GERMANY

Bundesverband Deutscher
Unternehmensberater (BDU) E.V.
Friedrich-Wilhelm-Strasse 2
5300 Bonn 1

GREECE

Hellenic Association
of Management
Consulting Firms
PO Box 61085
151 24 Marousi
Athens

HONG KONG

The Hong Kong Management
Association
Management House, 3rd Floor
26 Canal Road
Hong Kong

HUNGARY

Association of Management
Consultants in Hungary
c/o SZENZOR
PO Box 33
1363 Budapest

ICELAND

Felag Islenskra Rekstrarradgjafa
(FIRR)
c/o Icelandic Management
Association
Ananaustum 15
PB 760
Reykjavik

INDIA

Institute of Management
Consultants of India
Centre One, 11th Floor
Cuffe Parade
Bombay 400 005

INDONESIA

Ikatan Nasional Konsultan
Indonesia
Jl. Bendungan Hilir Raya No. 29
Jakarta 10210

IRELAND

Association of Management
Consulting Organisations (AMCO)
Confederation House
Kildare Street
Dublin 2

ITALY

Associazione Fra Società e Studi di
Consulenza di Direzione e Orga-
nizzazione Aziendale (ASSCO)
Via San Paolo 10
20121 Milan

Associazione Professionale dei Consulenti di Direzione e Organizzazione Aziendale (APCO)
Corso Venezia 49
20121 Milan

JAPAN

All Japan Federation of Management Organizations (Zennoren)
Kyoritsu Building
3-1-22 Shibakoen
Minato-ku
Tokyo 105

Association of Management Consultants in Japan
Shuwashibakoen Sanchome Building
3-1-38 Shiba Park
Minato-Ku
Tokyo 105

Chusho Kigyo Shindan Kyokai (Smaller Enterprise Consultants Association)
Ginza Section of MITI
6-15-1, Cinza, Chuo-ku
Tokyo 104

Meikokukai, Japan Productivity Center
3-1-1, Shibuya, Shibuya-ku
Tokyo 150

MALAYSIA

Institute of Management Consultants
10th Floor, MUI Plaza
Letter Box 63
Jalan P. Ramlee
Kuala Lumpur 50250

MEXICO

Asociación Mexicana de Empresas de Consultoria (AMEC)
calz. Legaria 252
Mexico City 17, DF

NETHERLANDS

Orde Van Organisatiekundigen en-Adviseurs
Koningslaan 34
1075 AD Amsterdam

Raad van Organisatie-Adviesbureau (ROA)
34 Van Stolkweg
PO Box 84200
2508 The Hague

NEW ZEALAND

Institute of Management Consultants New Zealand Incorporated
PO Box 2347
Auckland 1

NIGERIA

Institute of Management Consultants
14 Kagoro Close
PO Box 9194
Kaduna

Nigerian Association of Management Consultants
c/o Centre for Management Development
PO Box 7648, Ikorodu Road
Lagos

NORWAY

Norsk Forening av Radgivere i Bedriftsledelse
c/o Hartmark-Iras
PB 50
1324 Lysaker

PAKISTAN

National Association of Consultants of Pakistan (NACOP)
PO Box 8901
103-B, SMCH Society
Karachi

PHILIPPINES
Institute of Management
Consultants
c/o Mr. A. Figueras
PO Box 589
Manila

POLAND
Association of Economic
Consultants
Gorskiego 1, Apt. 3
00033 Warsaw

PORTUGAL
Associação Portuguesa de
Projectistas e Consultores (APPC)
Av. Antonio Augusto
  Aguiar 126-7°
1000 Lisbon

ROMANIA
Association of Management Con-
sultants in Romania (AMCOR)
10L Patrascanu
Bucharest 74671

RUSSIAN FEDERATION
Association of Consultants in
Economics and Management
c/o VNESHCONSULT
Podsosenskii pereulok 20/12
Moscow 107067

SINGAPORE
Institute of Management
Consultants
c/o 9 Penang Road
13-20 Park Mall
Singapore 0923

SLOVAKIA
Slovak Association for
Management Consulting
Viedenská cesta 5
852 20 Bratislava

SLOVENIA
Association of Management
Consultants of Slovenia
Slovenska c. 41
61000 Ljubljana

SOUTH AFRICA
Institute of Management Consul-
tants of Southern Africa
PO Box 784-305
Sandton 2146

SPAIN
Asociación Española de Empresas
de Ingeniería y Consultoras
(TECNIBERIA)
Velasquez 94
Aptdo 14 863
28006 Madrid

SWEDEN
Svenska Organisationkonsulters
Förening (SOK)
Box 7470
10392 Stockholm

SWITZERLAND
Association suisse des conseils en
organisation et gestion (ASCO)
c/o Aura AG
Mühlebachstrasse 28
8008 Zurich

TURKEY
Turkish Management Consultant
Firms Association
Gümussuyu Cad
44-4 Taksim
Istanbul

UNITED KINGDOM
Institute of Management
Consultants
5th Floor, 32/33 Hatton Garden
London EC1N 8DL

Management Consultancies
Association (MCA)
11 West Halkin Street
London SW1X 8JL

UNITED STATES

Academy of Management,
Managerial Consultation Division
c/o Joe Weiss
Management Department,
Bentley College
Waltham, Massachusetts 02254

American Institute of Certified
Public Accountants (AICPA),
Management Services Division
1211 Avenue of Americas
New York, NY 10036

Association of Internal Manage-
ment Consultants (AIMC)
Box 304
East Bloomfield, NY 14443

Association of Management
Consulting Firms (ACME)
(division of CCO)
521 Fifth Avenue, 35th Floor
New York, NY 10175

Council of Consulting
Organizations, Inc. (CCO)
521 Fifth Avenue, 35th Floor
New York, NY 10175

Institute of Management Con-
sultants (IMC) (division of CCO)
521 Fifth Avenue, 35th Floor
New York, NY 10175

2. International associations (consulting and related professions)

AFRICA

Federation of African Consultants
(FEAC/FECA)
01 PO Box 1387
01 Abidjan
Côte-d'Ivoire

EUROPE

European Committee of Consult-
ing Engineering Firms (CEBI)
103 Bd. de Waterloo
1000 Brussels

European Computing Services
Association (ESCA)
79-81 avenue de Cortenberg
1040 Brussels

European Federation of
Management Consulting
Associations (FEACO)
79 avenue de Cortenberg
1040 Brussels

European Foundation for
Management Development
(EFMD)
40 rue Washington
1050 Brussels

Féderation des experts comptables
européens (FEE)
83 rue de la Loi
1040 Brussels

LATIN AMERICA

Federación Latinoamericana de
Asociaciones de Consultores
(FELAC)
Suipacha 552 - Piso 4° - Of. 1
1008 Buenos Aires
Argentina

INTERNATIONAL

International Council of Manage-
ment Consulting Institutes (ICMCI)
32/33 Hatton Garden
London EC1N 8DL
United Kingdom

International Federation of
Accountants
540 Madison Avenue
New York, NY 10022
United States

International Federation of
Consulting Engineers (FIDIC)
PO Box 86
1000 Lausanne 12 Chailly
Switzerland

3. Selected international organizations

African Development Bank (AfDB)
PO Box 1387
Abidjan 01
Côte d'Ivoire

Asian Development Bank (ADB)
PO Box 789
Manila 2800
Philippines

**European Bank for Reconstruction
and Development (EBRD)**
122 Leadenhall Street
London EC3V 4QL
United Kingdom

**European Economic Communities
(EEC)**
200 Rue de la Loi
1049 Brussels
Belgium

**Inter-American Development Bank
(IDB)**
808 17th Street NW
Washington, DC 20577
United States

**International Chamber of Commerce
(ICC)**
38 Cour Albert 1er
75008 Paris
France

**International Finance Corporation
(IFC)**
1818 H Street NW
Washington, DC 20433
United States

**International Labour Organization
(ILO)**
4 route des Morillons
1211 Geneva 22
Switzerland

International Monetary Fund (IMF)
700 19th Street NW
Washington, DC 20431
United States

**International Organization of
Employers (IOE)**
28 chemin de Joinville
1216 Cointrin GE
Switzerland

**United Nations Development
Programme (UNDP)**
PO Box 1608
Grand Central Station
New York, NY 10163
United States

**United Nations Food and Agriculture
Organization (FAO)**
Via delle Terme di Caracalla
00100 Rome
Italy

**United Nations Industrial Develop-
ment Organization (UNIDO)**
PO Box 300
1400 Vienna
Austria

World Bank
1818 H Street NW
Washington, DC 20433
United States

USEFUL INFORMATION SOURCES ON MANAGEMENT CONSULTING

1. Selected books, reports and newsletters

Association of Management Consulting Firms. *How to select and use management consultants* (New York, 1987)

Consultants News (a monthly newsletter of the profession published by Kennedy Publications, Fitzwilliam, New Hampshire)

"The Economist survey of management consultancy" (*The Economist*, 13 Feb. 1988)

"The Financial Times survey of management consultancy" (published from time to time as a special section of *Financial Times*, e.g. on 15 May 1991)

International Federation of Consulting Engineers. *The White Book Guide, with other notes on documents for consultancy agreements* (Lausanne, 1991)

Kennedy Publications. *Management consulting 1990: The state of the profession* (Fitzwilliam, New Hampshire, 1990)

Kubr, M. (ed.): *Management consulting: A guide to the profession* (Geneva, ILO, second (revised) ed., 1986)

Markham, C. *Practical consulting* (London, Institute of Management Consultants, 1987)

Margerison, Ch. *Managerial consulting skills: A practical guide* (Aldershot, Hampshire, Gower, 1988)

Schein, E. *Process consultation*, Vol. II: *Lessons for managers and consultants* (Reading, Massachusetts, Addison-Wesley, 1987)

Weinberg, G. *The secrets of consulting* (New York, Dorset House, 1985)

World Bank. *Guidelines for the use of consultants by World Bank borrowers and by the World Bank as executing agency* (Washington, DC, 1981)

Sample form of contract for consultants' services (Washington, DC, 1989)

2. Directories

Consultants and consulting organisations directory 1990, 2 vols. (Detroit, Michigan, Gale Research Co., 10th ed., 1989)

Dick, N. *Directory of management consultants in the UK* (London, Task Force PRO LIBRA, 8th ed., 1991)

European directory of management consultants (London, Task Force PRO LIBRA, 1992)

The directory of management consultants (Fitzwilliam, New Hampshire, Kennedy Publications; periodically)

The directory of executive recruiters 1992 (Fitzwilliam, New Hampshire, Kennedy Publications; periodically)

European consultants directory (Detroit, Michigan, Gale Research Co., 1992)

FEACO directory (Brussels, European Federation of Management Consulting Associations, 1991)

Directories issued by national consultants' associations are not listed. They can be obtained from the addresses given in Appendix 1.

3. Agencies for locating consultants

Consultants News
(Jim Kennedy, Kennedy Publications)
Templeton Rd., Fitzwilliam, New Hampshire 03447, United States
Phone (603) 585-6544, Fax (603) 585-9555.

Jim Kennedy, publisher of *Consultants News*, directories and other sources on management consulting and executive search, helps informally, and free of charge, to establish contacts between consultants and clients. He would ask the potential client for as much information as possible on the nature of the assignment, anticipated budget, past experience with consultants, the sort of consulting firm that might be appropriate according to the client, etc. Then he tries to identify a few consulting firms that seem to fill the bill, contacts them to describe the situation without revealing the prospective client's name, checks the consultant's interest and experience, and identifies the partners who should be contacted. This information is conveyed to the client. As there is no charge, both the client and the consultant who may eventually do the job are expected to give feedback on what actually happens.

Management Consulting Information Service
(Anne Malach)
38 Blenheim Avenue,
Gants Hill, Ilford, Essex IG2 6JQ, United Kingdom
Phone (081) 554-4695

The Service runs a register of management consultants, including some 180-200 names. Any consultant can register (for a fee) and has to provide details of past clients from whom the service may obtain confidential reference. Any public or private organization can request free information since the service is funded by the consultants. The service provides short-lists for specific assignments, as well as general information on how consultants operate.

British Consultants Bureau
1 Westminster Palace Gardens, 1-7 Artillery Row,
London SW1P 1RI, United Kingdom
Phone (071) 222-3651, Fax (071) 222-3664

The Bureau aims to promote the interests of member firms in exporting their services. Therefore, its directory and information service are intended primarily for foreign clients. It also informs about business and management consulting services of engineering, energy, transport and similar agencies and firms.

GENIOS Wirtschaftsdatabanken
Postfach 1102, D-4000 Düsseldorf 1, Germany
Phone (0211) 887-1521, Fax (0211) 887-1520

GENIOS operates a computerized data bank on German management consultants, members of the BDU. The codes are BDUA for addresses and BDUB for firm profiles.

4. Regional and country surveys of management consulting services

ALPHA Publications
66 Seeleys Road, Beaconsfield,
Bucks HP9 1TB, United Kingdom
Phone (0494) 675-942, Fax (0494) 670-807

Ken Dawson, the founder of ALPHA Publications, produces and distributes special regional and country reports on the market for management consulting services, trends in consulting and important management consulting firms. He has issued major reports on the United States, Japan and, most recently (1992), on Western Europe. Other reports will be forthcoming. These reports provide fairly detailed information on the profiles, activities and services of leading consulting firms active in each region and country covered.

THE 24 LARGEST INTERNATIONAL MANAGEMENT CONSULTING FIRMS

Name	No. of consultants	Main country base	Comments on profile
1. Andersen Consulting	21,600	United States (48%)	• Multifunctional • Information technology and systems • Operations, manufacturing, logistics • Sales and marketing • One of Big Six
2. Mercer Consulting Group	7,900 (all employees)	United States (65%)	• Conglomerate • Employee benefits • Compensation • Formerly Marsh and McLellan
3. Price Waterhouse	7,200	United States (41%)	• Multifunctional • Sector specialization • Information technology • One of Big Six
4. Coopers & Lybrand (in United Kingdom: Coopers Lybrand Deloitte)	7,000	United States (43%)	• Multifunctional • Information technology • Actuarial, benefits • Operations, distribution, manufacturing • One of Big Six
5. Ernst and Young	6,300	United States (64%)	• Multifunctional • Information technology • Operations, productivity • Finance, banking • One of Big Six (merger of Ernst & Whinney and Arthur Young in 1989)
6. KPMG	5,900	United States (44%) and Netherlands	• Multifunctional • Banking • General management • Loose association of firms • One of Big Six
7. Deloitte Touche Ross (in UK: Touche Ross; internationally: DRT)	5,300	United States (59%)	• Multifunctional • Information technology • Finance • Operations • One of Big Six (merger of Touche Ross and Deloitte Haskins & Sells in 1989)
8. Towers Perrin	3,500	United States (71%)	• Strategy and organization • Actuarial • Benefits, compensation

Name	No. of consultants	Main country base	Comments on profile
9. CSC Consulting	3,400	United States (56%)	• Conglomerate • Information technology • Systems development and integration
10. American Management Systems	3,100	United States (91%)	• Information technology • Computer systems and management
11. Booz-Allen & Hamilton	3,100	United States (75%)	• Technology • Strategy • Industry sector specialization • Manufacturing and distribution • Productivity
12. Noble Lowndes	2,700	United Kingdom	• Benefits, compensation
13. McKinsey	2,600	United States (40%)	• General management • Strategy, organization • Finance • Strong research base
14. Wyatt Co.	2,300	United States (76%)	• Human resource management • Benefits • Risk and insurance management • Strong research base
15. Hewitt Associates	2,100	United States (93%)	• Benefits, compensation • Focus on manufacturing and services
16. Gemini Consulting	1,700	France	• Information technology
17. PA Consulting	1,600	United Kingdom	• Multifunctional • Information technology • Manufacturing and logistics • Technology management • Telecommunications
18. Arthur D. Little	1,500	United States (56%)	• Sector studies and consulting • Strategy and organization • Technology management • Operations • Environment, health
19. Alexander Consulting Group	1,400	United States (70%)	• Actuarial, benefits, compensation • Human resource management
20. A. Foster Higgins	1,200	United States (80%)	• Employee benefits, compensation
21. Buck Consultants	1,100	United States (75%)	• Pension and employee benefits • Health and welfare
22. Alexander Proudfoot	1,100	United States (67%)	• Efficiency, cost cutting • Production, operations • Quality management

Name	No. of consultants	Main country base	Comments on profile
23. PE International	1,100	United Kingdom	• Multifunctional • Manufacturing, oil, gas and chemicals • Information technology • Retail, distribution • Public sector
24. Hay Group	1,000	United States (40%)	• Multifunctional • Human resource management • Job evaluation, compensation

Source: Information from *Consultants News* (June 1992) and other sources.

INDEX
